Visual Design
with OSF/Motif™

Hewlett-Packard Press Series

Shiz Kobara

Visual Design
with OSF/Motif™

 **HEWLETT PACKARD**

▲▼ **Addison-Wesley Publishing Company, Inc.**

Reading, Massachusetts • Menlo Park, California • New York
Don Mills, Ontario • Wokingham, England • Amsterdam
Bonn • Paris • Milan • Madrid • Sydney • Singapore
Tokyo • Seoul • Taipei • Mexico City • San Juan

Many of the designations used by manufacturers and sellers to distinguish their products are claimed as trademarks. Where those designations appear in this book and Addison-Wesley was aware of a trademark claim, the designations have been printed in initial caps (i.e., Symphony).

The programs and applications presented in this book have been included for their instructional value. They have been tested with care, but are not guaranteed for any particular purpose. The publisher does not offer any warranties or representations, nor does it accept any liabilities with respect to the programs or applications.

Library of Congress Cataloging-in-Publication Data

Kobara, Shiz.
    Visual design with OSF/Motif / Shiz Kobara
      p.   cm
      Includes bibliographical references and index.
      ISBN 0–201–56320–7
      1. Windows (Computer programs) 2. Motif (Computer program)
I. Title.
QA76.76.W56K63 1991   91–2449
005.4'3—dc20   CIP

The publisher offers discounts on this book when ordered in quantity for special sales. For more information please
contact:
    Corporate & Professional Publishing Group
    Addison-Wesley Publishing Company
    One Jacob Way
    Reading, Massachusetts   01867

Cover design by Shiz Kobara

Text design by Melinda Grosser for *silk*

Set in 10 point Palatino by Miracle Type

ISBN 0–201–56320–7

Printed on recycled and acid-free paper.

Second Printing, December 1991
2 3 4 5 6 7 8 9–AL–9594939291

To my wife Kathy

Contents

Acknowledgments

Many people were involved in the development of this book, either directly by reviewing the many drafts or indirectly through discussions regarding Motif's visual design. Several drafts were sent out during the development of this book and the time spent by the following people in reviewing each draft is greatly appreciated. With hopes that I am not missing anyone, thank you to Steve Anderson, Bob Desinger, Oliver Jones, Bob May, Vish Narayanan, Keith Taylor, and Doug Young, who through their technical and visual design knowledge have continuously contributed to improving this book throughout its development. Their many suggestions and critical reviews have helped immensely to improve this book and communicate this material in the best way possible.

Thank you to Lougenia Anderson, Matt Avery, Mark Avery, Alka Badshah, Douglas Blewett, Jennifer Chaffee, Ken Flowers, Eviatar 'Ev' Shafrir, Phil Tuchinsky, and Rainer Wieland, all of whom have reviewed the book's drafts in part or in whole. Their many suggestions have helped to improve the book's content.

For their patience with my never-ending questions, thanks go to Nick Baer, Ben Ellsworth, Molly Joy, Rick McKay, Julie Skeen, Jason Su, Joseph Whitty, and Jennefer Wood. They have always been there to answer my urgent technical questions.

Thank you to the management of Hewlett Packard—Chuck House, Steve Joseph, Chung Tung, Ted Wilson, John Brewster, Bob Miller, Brock Krizan, Ione Crandell, Bob Merritt, and Ray Fajardo—for their full support in this effort.

Thank you to Brenda Kufer, who has energetically administered this project throughout its development.

Everyone needs a coach, especially if it is the first time that they are tackling a project. Special thanks go to my manager and coach, Barry Mathis, who has championed this book from its inception. Through his wisdom, Barry has guided me through this project on a clear course for 12 exciting and exhausting months.

Last but certainly not the least, my greatest thanks go to my wife Kathy, who believed in me and cheerfully put up with my long nights and entire weekends at the computer. I could not have finished this book without her.

I would like to also thank Kathryn Birkbeck, Ellis Cohen, and Craig Lamont of the Open Software Foundation for their support of this book. Thank you to everyone at Addison-Wesley, particularly John Wait, who had the foresight to believe in this project from the beginning and who has always been there to lead me through this; Kathleen Manley, who handled all of the reviews; Ted Buswick, who started this project with me; Alan Apt, who helped put closure onto this project; Perry McIntosh, who with her magic turned this into a real book; and Kim Dawley and Vivian Sudhalter, who will be marketing this book. I would also like to thank everyone at HP Press who has created this rare opportunity for me to be able to publish this book under the HP Press banner, particularly Dick Alberding, Jan Staumbach, and Bob Silvey.

Thanks, finally, to Brian Holt, who gave me the idea for writing this book.

Throughout the entire book, any examples or information that are in error are my responsibility alone.

Shiz Kobara

Foreword

This book is for people who want to design more appealing and more useful computer screen interfaces for human operators. It is unique in its approach, insightful for the serious student, while readable and useful for the novice. Shiz Kobara and several colleagues at Hewlett-Packard have strong backgrounds in user interface design experience based on industrial design and human factors. Kobara has captured for the reader much of the lore of these separate disciplines as it applies to the visual design of applications using OSF/Motif.

A bit of historical perspective may help to position the need for this book. Our age has been one of mankind adapting to computers. As we entered 1980, there were about a half-million computers in America, which were mostly used in industry. By 1990, there were 50,000,000, of which one half are located in homes. Ninety-five percent of the users of these computers have word processing and spreadsheet software that have better user interfaces than virtually any software available for these tasks ten years ago.

Computer scientists, by and large, have been creating and learning new computer interfaces using the mnemonic approach. As a result, users of MS/DOS™ know that *A:* means "Root Directory, Disk Drive 'A'", and UNIX hackers type GREP when they want to "Globally find Regular Expressions and Print." These mnemonics, or abbreviations, can be quite efficient when learned. But novice users often have difficulty using mnemonics. Some computing visionaries saw the need for a better computer interface. In the early 1960s, pioneers such as Doug Englebart began research on Graphical User Interfaces, or GUIs, in the hope of expanding the usability of computers beyond the limited circle of those people with the time and resources to learn mnemonic interfaces.

Silicon Valley was a particularly fertile area for computing interfaces in the early 1980s. Englebart's ideas were greatly expanded at Xerox's Palo Alto Research Center (PARC), by visionaries including Alan Kay. Atari created simple interfaces for children's games that demystified computer power for many people.

By 1980, HP Laboratories' collaboration with PARC on experiments with the Smalltalk environment signaled a shift in HP's machine interface efforts to user interface questions. By the latter half of the '80s, HP software engineers began coordinating their efforts with Shiz Kobara and other interface designers to improve the user interface for all HP software products. Shiz's book represents the best effort to date to codify the results of this subtle learning about interface design.

We believed we could build upon much of the thinking about computer screen icons and "field" location, and add our own knowledge of application-domain specialties with both visual design and human factors principles to develop a significant improvement in both the appeal and usability of computer interfaces by "lay users."

Thus, the true purpose of this book is to help many new screen designers build excellent designs. The consequences will be significant for you as a designer if you learn, study, and use these principles based on the Motif 3D look and feel. OSF selected the Motif 3D appearance and behavior over 42 entries and it was selected by *BYTE Magazine* as the Software User Interface product of the year in 1990.

The message, we believe, is these design rules can give you a head start in designing more effective screens for applications and users in all computing fields. It is an exciting time as well for industrial designers in computing for it signals the acknowledgment of the value of these disciplines. Shiz Kobara has tried to empower you with this book by sharing the lore and secrets of user interface design. Best wishes, then, as you learn the subtle, but vital craft of visual design with OSF/Motif.

Charles H. House, Hewlett-Packard Company
Palo Alto, California
May 1991

Preface

The subject of Graphical User Interfaces (GUI) has gained much attention in the computer software industry within the past few years. There are many examples on the market, such as Xerox with its Star™, Apple with its Macintosh® , AT&T with Open Look® , and Microsoft with its MS Windows™. These GUIs are comprised of user interface components designed for intuitive direct manipulation. In the OSF/Motif ™ GUI, these components are called *widgets*. These widgets have to be assembled so that the resultant layout is visually pleasing as well as logical for the end user. Many long hours are devoted not only to the functional coding of an application's interface but also to its graphical design and layout. This latter task has typically been left to software engineers, sometimes with some help from an artist or a designer. The Motif GUI doesn't make this task any easier. The Motif GUI, in fact, can be quite a challenge to configure if the application developer doesn't have a clear mental picture of Motif's visual components. Its visually three-dimensional nature requires that attention be paid to many more subtle details than in past two-dimensional GUIs. Any help in visualizing an interface layout that uses Motif, however, can lead to aesthetically pleasing and predictable results. Motif's visual complexity, if understood, can ultimately result in visually compelling application interfaces.

Motif is designed to be thoroughly three-dimensional, both visually and behaviorally. With its visual three-dimensionality comes real-world three-dimensional behavior. Pushbuttons appear to push in when pressed, Scrollbars glide in channels, and Menupanes appear to leap out of the Menubar onto the application area. All this real-world behavior has one major drawback for the application developer using Motif. Motif inherently contains more visual components that require configuration when compared with a visually two-dimensional interface scheme. This requires more work for the application developer in having to remember and understand these concepts. There are simply more different combinations of colors, fonts, and widget sizes than there ever were in past two-dimensional graphical user interfaces. The results, however, can be visually and behaviorally compelling compared with previous GUIs.

Things can easily go wrong as well in Motif. The results can be disastrous, not to mention frustrating and discouraging to the application developer who has spent long hours picking what were thought to be the correct colors, widget spacing, and font selection. I have seen examples in developing and working with Motif where a slight color difference or font size variation can make for a visually awkward interface.

This book will explain, with visual examples, the concept and design philosophy of the Motif three-dimensional interface. It is intended as a guidebook for software engineers and graphical interface designers to visualize the optimum design potential of Motif. It explains the artistic theory of achieving the three-dimensional illusion and how that principle pervades the design of every widget component in Motif. This book also explains, with visual examples, the construction of all widgets and their layout policies. A person wanting to try out these policies can do so using a system that supports Motif, or even by mocking up these interface concepts with a bitmapped paint program. Motif provides a set of widgets that serves as a foundation for visually exciting user interface designs. This book also serves as a guide to the fundamental principles of the unique visual properties of Motif. With this book as a guide and Motif as an interface foundation, an application developer can be freed up to concentrate on more important issues, such as achieving creative and task-specific results using Motif.

This book also will touch on what to think about when designing new applications employing direct manipulation graphical interfaces. This is not a style guide of OSF's Motif interface, nor is it meant to be a programmatic reference manual for layout design. There are other books that explain those subjects in greater detail. This book is intended to describe the visual component makeup of OSF/Motif's widgets so that a better understanding of the interface's visual design potential can be realized. It is intended to also help software designers and developers understand OSF/Motif's complex visual model.

This book by no means replaces an artist or a trained professional interface designer. These professionals provide a wealth of design and ergonomic experience that is not possible to cover in a book. With the aid of this book, however, an interface designer can help with the creative visual design of applications based on OSF/Motif.

Overview

This book is written from a user interface and visual design perspective. It explains the subtle visual design details that are encountered in using Motif and illustrates the adjustable visual components of each widget. As a practicing user interface designer, I have written this book from my experience in working with software engineers in developing Motif's visual components as well as other products, such as HP's "Softbench" and HP's VUE (Visual User Environment).

This book is divided into two major sections. The first section, chapters 1 through 6, describes Motif's visual components, including widgets, color, fonts, window manager, and icons. The second section covers visual design principles and guidelines, including what to think about before attempting to start designing an application, proper visual layouts of widgets in applications, application and dialog box design layouts, and some examples of conceptual designs based on Motif that can help stretch your imagination to the design possibilities of Motif's visual model.

Motif's Visual Components

Chapter 1   The Motif Three-Dimensional Design Philosophy:
This chapter summarizes a brief history of the development of the
three-dimensional GUI (Graphical User Interface) that eventually has
come to be known as OSF/Motif. It explains the fundamental reasons behind Motif's visual design, including establishment of the
lighting model, the reasons for top and bottom shadows, and the pervasive three-dimensional visual design goal that was ultimately
achieved.

Chapter 2   Color: This chapter discusses the effect that Motif's widgets have on color space. Understanding this concept is helpful before you assign colors to your interface. Because of Motif's complex set
of visual components in each widget, careful use of color is required
in order not to run out of color space in your system.

Chapter 3   Fonts: This chapter discusses the effect that fonts have
on almost every widget in Motif. It is helpful to understand this concept before assigning fonts to your widgets. Through our experience, fonts are one of the key elements in your interface that affect
the appearance and clarity of your interface.

Chapter 4   Widgets: This chapter describes the visual properties of
every visible widget in OSF/Motif. A clear understanding of the component makeup of these widgets can be gained from this chapter.
This chapter is divided into subsections for every widget for easier access to each widget's visual specifications.

Chapter 5   Window Manager: This chapter explains the choices in
window frame appearance that are available to the application designer.

Chapter 6   Icons: This chapter explains the role of the icon as well
as describing the different types of icon styles that we have used in
Motif. Also explained are some techniques that can be employed to
achieve compelling icon images.

Motif's Visual Design Principles

Chapter 7   Design Principles: This chapter discusses what you
should think about before designing an application interface. Initial
research of your market using the basic steps in this chapter will help
keep you focused on your audience when designing an application
interface.

Chapter 8   Application Design Guidelines: This chapter covers aesthetic layout guidelines that will make your applications look consistent and appealing. Also covered is the basic visual placement of widgets in an application that will make it Motif-compliant. Examples of existing applications based on Motif are included.

Chapter 9   Dialog Box Design Guidelines: This chapter covers basic visual placement of widgets in a dialog box. It also explains what to think about when designing dialog boxes so that its visual layout clearly displays its specific functions. Examples of existing dialog boxes based on Motif are included.

Chapter 10   Where Are We Headed?: This chapter discusses the visual design potential that is possible with OSF/Motif. New technologies that will be based on OSF/Motif become visual design problems in conveying their unique functionalities. Examples of conceptual designs of applications that are not yet available are included. This chapter is meant to discuss the design potential of new capabilities based on OSF/Motif's visual model.

Audience

This book is addressed to designers of applications using the OSF/Motif Graphical User Interface. Much of the material in this book can also be of interest to anyone who wants a better understanding of OSF/Motif's visual properties and design principles in designing user interfaces. This book assumes some familiarity with OSF/Motif and its resource files.

The *you* in this book refers to the reader. It is written for those who want to learn about recommended visual design principles. The term *user* in this book refers to the customer or end user of the application that you are designing for or are involved with. It is not intended to refer to "you" the application designer.

The *we* in this book refers to the user interface designers and engineers at HP who have designed and developed most of the visual design principles of Motif.

All illustrations reflect recommended appearance characteristics using OSF/Motif. Any illustrations intended to show bad or inappropriate use are shown with the international symbol for "no" (circle with a line through it).

Motif's Visual Components

The Motif Three-Dimensional
Design Philosophy

The OSF/Motif visual interface was conceived initially as an effort by Hewlett Packard to create a graphical user interface for the UNIX platform. One of the earliest directives of this interface was that it would adhere to IBM's CUA (Common User Access) behavioral standard to guarantee graphical user behavior consistency between UNIX and MS-DOS platforms. This effort was called CXI (Common X Interface) for use within HP. The three-dimensional visual character of HP's CXI interface was later adopted by the Open Software foundation as the standard visual appearance of their new GUI (Graphical User Interface). OSF had the HP CXI three-dimensional appearance incorporated with the functionality and API (Application Program Interface) of the widgets in the XUI (X User Interface) created by DEC (Digital Equipment Corporation). The result of this combined effort between HP and DEC has become Open Software Foundation's Motif graphical user interface.

Why Three-Dimensional?

From the outset we conducted an extensive analysis of interface types that were the current state of the art. We studied Apple's Macintosh, Sun's NeWS, Xerox's Star/Viewpoint, and Microsoft's MS Windows. Our conclusion from a visual design point of view was that these graphical interfaces were of a two-dimensional nature and were very successful in communicating a direct manipulation metaphor. We found that in searching for our own visual differentiator, we had the opportunity to explore various visual techniques. The one that most intrigued us was the notion of creating a three-dimensional illusion on the two-dimensional CRT.

After this initial research and a period of conceptualization of what our interface would look like, we were given the freedom to experiment with various visual concepts with multiple colors. The state of the art in hardware technology at HP was reaching the performance levels that would support multiple colors and also provided almost instantaneous redraw rates. This allowed us to explore even further. We started experimenting with color and drew from our industrial design and ergonomics experience to create a convincing visually and behaviorally three-dimensional set of components (widgets). By employing this three-dimensional design direction, we developed visual cues of what to expect in the way of interface behavior. Pushbuttons began to appear like rectangular protrusions that could be pressed. Text entry areas looked as though they were recessed into the surface of the background. The use of subtle color changes in the recessed areas indicates to the user whether the text within is for display only or for editing. Scrollbars were designed as troughs that appeared to be of the same depth as an editable window with a rectangular valuator gliding within. As we continued to explore the visual possibilities of this interface, we found that we had the technology to support a visually thorough and compelling three-dimensional illusion by employing some basic artistic techniques. Figure 1–1 shows early attempts at creating the three-dimensional illusion.

The goal of our CXI GUI, which at the time was also officially called in manuals "the HP X Widgets," was to emulate as much as possible, by visual and behavioral design, the appearance and actions of the real physical world. With the availability of sophisticated color systems, such as the ones we had at HP, the opportunity to explore a sophisticated design approach for this new interface became obvious. We felt that this would enhance the experience of manipulating the virtual environment presented on the screen. The design evolved into a scheme in which anything that was a part of the system interface would be visually three-dimensional and anything into which the user would type or draw would

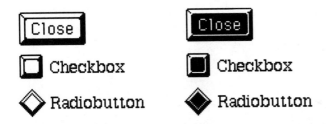

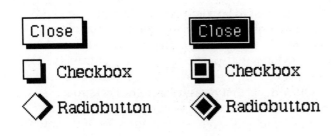

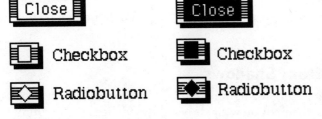

FIGURE 1–1 Early attempts at creating the three-dimensional illusion were done by delineating light and dark chamfers with only black and white onto two-dimensional-styled widgets. Various styles were employed, including explorations of rounded corners and drop shadows.

be visually two-dimensional in a recessed area. With this design direction set, we had a clear strategy of what would be an interface area and what would be a working area.

The Light Source

We established a convention of a perceived light source early in the development of CXI. The role of the light source was significant, because this was what determined where and how to place light and dark shadows. This in turn ultimately dictated how the colors were placed to give a convincing three-dimensional appearance.

The light source was determined to be coming from the upper left and from behind the left shoulder of the user when seated in front of a computer display. This dictated that every widget that protruded from the background surface was to have the appearance of being lit from the top and left. Consequently, everything that was on the right and bottom would be in shadow. On widgets that recessed into the background surface, these would be reversed. The body or background of the interface would be of a mid value and would serve as the main color of the interface component. This light source direction follows a historic convention for art and illustration being lit from the upper left.

This light source should remain constant throughout all interface components (widgets) that were to be designed. By employing this lighting model consistently throughout the design and development of the CXI widgets, we were able to ensure visual quality and eliminate any confusion that would have been caused by an inconsistent lighting model.

Top and Bottom Shadows

As a result of establishing the lighting model, a consistent system of placing light and dark shadows on widgets was defined. Because anything designed for Motif had to be of a rectilinear shape, we established this model for visual consistency in the early stages. This visual trick is now called *top and bottom shadows.* Essentially, every widget has a set of chamfers that make up the top and bottom shadows that surround it. These shadows can be colored according to the lighting model and reversed to appear as if the widget protrudes from or recedes into the background surface. Figure 1–2 shows top and bottom shadows protruding from and receding into the background.

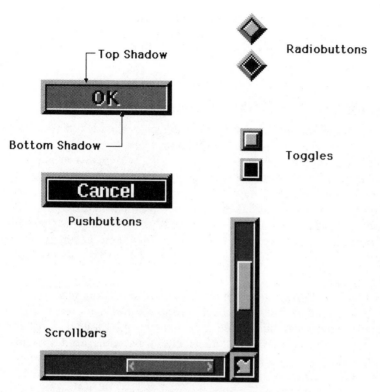

Early 3-D Top and Bottom Shadow Concept

FIGURE 1–2 These early-style examples of top and bottom shadows were done with a number of shades of gray. Exploration of font styles included an engraved look shown here. This concept was visually too complex and a simpler style was necessary.

We established a rule that for any rectangular shape that protruded, the top shadow (top and left chamfers) would be a lighter color of the background color and the bottom shadow (bottom and right chamfers) would be a darker version of the background color. This simple rule was applied to every widget designed to be either pushed or grabbed, such as a Pushbutton or a Scrollbar valuator. The concept of text entry and display areas, however, required the opposite rule. Areas that were recessed into the background required reversing the highlight and shadow colors, which made the top and left chamfers a darker version of the background color and the bottom and right chamfers a lighter version of the background color. This created a rectangular shape that looked as though it was recessed into the background. The result was subtle but convincing. The terms *top and bottom shadows* came to be used to describe the beveled frame that surrounds almost every widget.

Sculpting the Motif Slab Concept

Once these rules were understood and established, the idea of visually assembling the individual widgets posed a problem. Unlike the earlier two-dimensional interface style, in which the widgets were laid out on a white background with a border surrounding them, this three-dimensional effect created a new design problem. The challenge was to adhere these three-dimensional components in an all-inclusive manner that would provide a consistent look. With the knowledge that these interface components were to live in a multiwindowed environment, we felt that these widgets would have to be assembled onto a visual slab of some sort.

From early concepts we learned that the three-dimensional widgets placed against a two-dimensional background did not work well visually. The three-dimensional widgets looked as though they were lost and afloat on a background that lacked visual cues that would hold the widgets in place. We quickly learned that these three-dimensional elements did not look appropriate in a two-dimensional world. We determined that if this three-dimensional approach were to be successful, all elements in this new environment would have to employ the three-dimensional design direction. Figure 1–3 shows early three-dimensional widgets on a two-dimensional background, compared with the current Motif-style visual slab.

We introduced to the engineers the concept of a "slab" that would visually hold the widgets in place. This became the visual basis of Motif's widget background. A concept was established that all windows from a simple dialog box to a full-blown application window would require the "slab" appearance to adhere its widgets together visually in the background. This visual sculpting technique of the interface parts was adopted as one of the fundamental visual rules for the three-dimensional interface design. No widget will exist alone in space without a visual slab in this environment. The slab became known as the background of color upon which the widgets are placed. The background can be surrounded with a frame to give a "slab" look or flat background areas can be bordered by a window frame. The widgets are colored the same as the

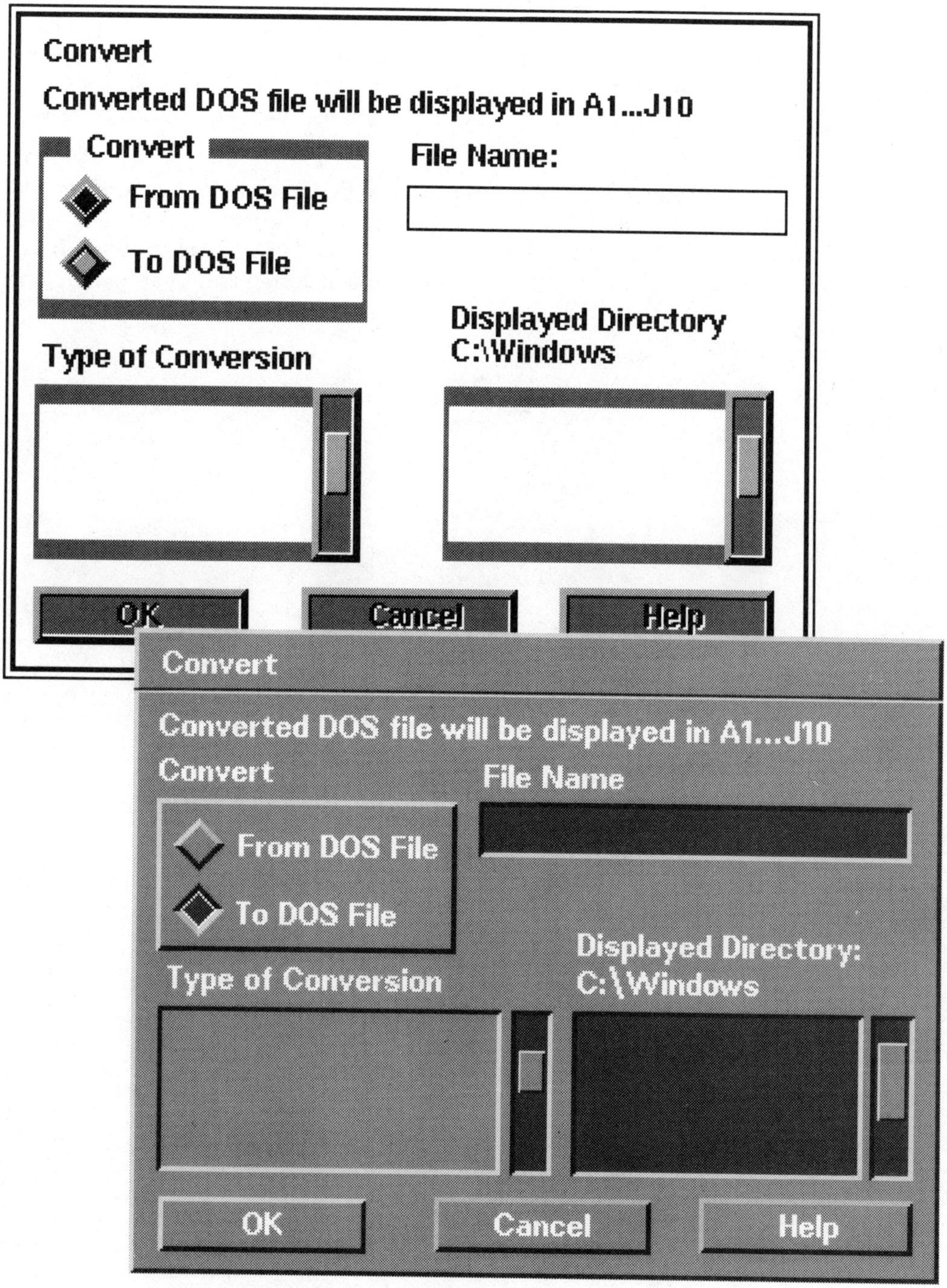

Convert

Converted DOS file will be displayed in A1...J10

Convert

◆ From DOS File

◆ To DOS File

File Name:

Type of Conversion

Displayed Directory
C:\Windows

OK   Cancel   Help

Convert

Converted DOS file will be displayed in A1...J10

Convert

◇ From DOS File

◆ To DOS File

File Name

Type of Conversion

Displayed Directory:
C:\Windows

OK   Cancel   Help

FIGURE 1–3 Early analysis of three-dimensional widgets revealed that these new widgets would have to be placed visually in other windows, such as this dialog box. This example shows how early three-dimensional widgets appeared awkward on a two-dimensional surface (top). The concept of the simple slab was then conceived (bottom).

background color to accentuate the three-dimensional look of protruding from the surface. The background also provides a visual area in which recessed areas are created by text entry widgets. Figure A–1 (color section) shows how HP's CXI widget design has evolved ultimately to become Motif.

The following chapters in this book will describe obvious as well as subtle visual details of Motif's GUI. As shown in figures A–2 and A–3 in the color section, paying attention to the visual details can mean the difference between a visually awkward interface design and a compelling one.

Motif's Colors

2

Chapter

No area in design is more subjective than that of color. Color can mean so many different things to different people. Color can convey warmth or coolness, relaxation or urgency. Color is a key element in fashion. One year's popular color can be next year's disaster. In many cultures, certain colors have significant meaning and should not be used casually in dress or in products, for they can often offend or connote radically diverse meanings. Color can show function as well as be used for decorative purposes. It can be used for coding purposes. *Color-coding* is a term that most of us have heard at one time or another in our lifetimes. Color can warn you of danger and can also show impending danger when used as a gradual warning. Color is used as expression and can be used whether you want to express loudly or quietly. Color is often judged as style and conveys certain information about your personality.

Our world is full of color, and the careful use of color can greatly enhance one's environment. Color, whether used for decorative or logical purposes, tells a great deal about the design of a product and can be used as a device to convey its functionality to the intended audience.

In the world of industrial design, color plays an important role in showing off an object's form. Color values (brightness level) have a great effect on how easily a form is read. An automobile body's form, for example, is much more easily discernible when painted in a light color such as white than when it is painted black. From an objective point of view, the reflections on light glossy surfaces are not as high in contrast and appear as subtle shades so the form reads easier. On the other hand, reflections on dark glossy surfaces tend to be of higher contrast and can distort or hide the form.

Color can be very subjective in products also. Some people may want a dark colored car over a light colored car because of personal preference. Black may seem more formal or sporty to some people; an equal number of people may think that white is more formal and sporty. White does not show dirt as readily; however, once daylight changes to darkness, black may show less dirt because of its high reflectivity. So color is a funny thing. It changes as quickly as the surrounding light changes. Color is one thing that people take for granted although they are highly affected by it.

The world of Motif is not much different in the use of color. Many people ask me what are good color combinations for widgets. My answer to them is that there are as many different opinions of what are good color combinations as there are people using Motif. My basic recommendation is to pick a color scheme that is pleasing to you for use for long periods of time. The colors you choose should provide enough contrast between the background color and the foreground (text or pixmap) color for easy clarity, without being too harsh, like white on black or black on white (unless, of course, you are using a monochrome display). Avoid combinations like blue on black or red on yellow. These are very harsh combinations, are very difficult to read, and will cause eye strain over long periods of time. I tend to favor the polychromatic neutral colors, such as teal, mauve, and medium grays, for background colors. These midrange tones will work fine and will offer enough contrast with white foreground text colors. There are also users who prefer a color scheme that is predominately one color, such as green or blue. From my experience, the colors you use should be comfortable for you.

The Role of Color in Motif

Motif was designed to take full advantage of the color capabilities that are becoming more and more available in workstation displays. And just as they must be used with care in the real world, colors must be applied carefully in the Motif environment. Color usage must be well planned in advance or you will either expend the available color space or not leave enough available for future applications that require vast amounts of color space, such as a graphics program.

The careful use of color in the Motif interface is what really brings to life its three-dimensional appearance. The use of subtle, medium-contrast colors rather than loud high-contrast colors is preferred in order to achieve a convincing and appealing three-dimensional look. Unless careful selection and use of color is incorporated into Motif, you can end up with a rather garish and often cartoonish visual quality in the appearance of your application interface. As in the real world, the different shades of the main background color that make up the top and bottom shadows are what provide the convincing 3-dimensional illusion. Figure A–4 (color section) shows examples of the types of loud, high-contrast colors that are not recommended for use in widget color.

You can give widgets their own colors independent of their parent color. For consistency and aesthetics, I recommend that widgets be assigned the same color as their parent. If gadgets are used, however, their background color is forced to match that of its parent widget. Though colors can be assigned in any combination that suits the particular application's design, some careful forethought and the development of a color strategy go a long way to achieving successful and predictable results. This is especially helpful if many applications are to share the same environment. Figure 2–1 shows a widget and its color components.

Color Map (How Widgets Eat Up Color Space)

First let's take a quick look at how the color server works in X. In this example we will use a 6-bit color display card. A 6-bit card will display 64 colors at a time. In color display technology, each bit equals a power of 2; therefore, in this example, a 6-bit card equals 2 to the power of 6, or 64. Thus, we are allowed 64 color cells in this environment. Most color displays in use today incorporate an 8-bit color display card and can display 256 colors. Some can even display more colors than that. For this example, I will refer to the 6-bit card for several reasons. This is the card for which we had to design widget color sets, and it will illustrate just how quickly Motif widgets can eat up color space if you are restricted to only 64 color cells. Color efficiency can be used as well on systems that display more than 64 colors. Hopefully, you will have access to more color cells than this when using Motif.

The color map works on a first-come, first-served basis for assigning application color requirements. These 64 cells have no colors in them until the application is launched and tells the server what colors it needs in

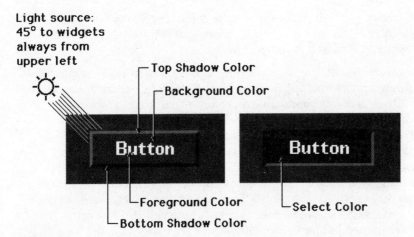

Light source: 45° to widgets always from upper left

— Top Shadow Color

— Background Color

Button   Button

—Foreground Color   —Select Color

—Bottom Shadow Color

FIGURE 2–1 Motif's widget color components are designed to look as though the light source is positioned 45 degrees from the upper left. The angle of the light source remains consistent throughout the Motif GUI.

order to display itself on the screen. As applications are launched, each with its own color requirements, the color map obliges these requests and continues to fill up its 64 cells. It will continue to grant new color cells to any new color requests. At the same time, it will share color cells for any requests of an existing color. The server will assign color cells as needed until all 64 color cells are filled. After these spaces are filled up and another application is launched, requesting any new colors, the color map server will conduct a search for the nearest comparable colors for the application's particular color needs. This search will be conducted only if the new application was designed with that feature. The color map server will assign the closest match for that color request for this type of application. If, however, the application was not designed with this feature of color approximation, the server will default all light colors to white and all dark colors to black. This will make the incoming application look disastrous. Figure 2–2 shows a graphical representation of a 64-color map.

The color map can reserve only two colors permanently: black and white. So, a 64-color space color map can actually hold only 62 colors. For 256 color systems, this means that 254 colors are available. The color map will reserve colors that are required to be displayed. It will also remember colors that were specified previously by an application. As long as there are enough color cells available, the color map will continue to remember a specified color in a given cell even though that particular application has since been closed and is no longer referring to that color. If, however, the color map spaces become filled to capacity, the color cells

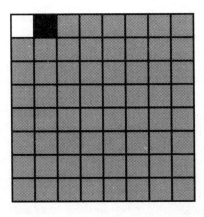

64 Color Map

FIGURE 2–2 An example of how I picture a 64-color map when thinking about how many colors are being used.

that have been previously assigned a color, but that are currently not being referred to for display, will be reassigned a new color at the request of any new applications requiring its specific colors. The color map is concerned only with which colors you need at any one time to be displayed on the screen rather than how many you need total for other applications that are not displayed.

Most monitors promise the ability to display almost 16 million colors these days, but remember that the type of display card you use will determine the total amount of colors that will be displayed at any one time. Monitors also vary in color consistency. This is true even between identical models from the same manufacturer. Therefore, you are not guaranteed absolute consistency in the colors that you have developed for a certain application.

Color Sets

Motif's three-dimensional appearance affects the number of colors that are required in creating Motif's interfaces. Each widget requires four colors, or color spaces as defined by the color server. They are the top shadow, background, select color, and bottom shadow colors. These are the main color components of each widget that are involved in creating the three-dimensional illusion. The foreground color used for the label in some widgets is displayed as either black or white. The following will describe each color component of the widget color set. Figure A–5 (color section) shows the different colors necessary for displaying a widget and its color set.

Motif incorporates a very good color algorithm that will automatically calculate the correct top and bottom shadows and select colors based on the widget's background color. This algorithm adjusts the value (brightness) based on the widget's background color to achieve the proper top and bottom shadows and select color. This algorithm will also determine when to flip the foreground color from black to white depending on the amount of contrast of the foreground color when compared to the brightness of its background color. This flipping of the foreground color will ensure good contrast between the foreground and the background colors. Although Motif takes care of these other color components of every widget, it is a good idea to understand the concept behind the color set. The following will describe the concept behind how the select color and top and bottom shadows were derived. This can be handy if you ever need to assign these colors manually.

Background Color

The background color is the main color of the widgets and the background on which they are positioned. It should be the color that is decided upon first when designing an application and that is used for color compatibility when deciding on a scheme of colors. The background color is the main color that is most visible in an application and is the color base upon which all the other color components (top and bottom shadows and the select color) are derived.

The ideal background colors should be in the mid-range of the RGB (Red, Green, & Blue) scale of colors. They should not be too bright or too dark. A bright background will cause the top shadow not to be very visible because both background color and top shadow will be very bright. A dark background color will cause the bottom shadow to be very dark and not visible against the dark background color. The visible contrast between the background color and its top and bottom shadows are what create the visual three-dimensional illusion of these widgets. The mid-range of RGB brightness that seems to work the best is 155 to 175 on a 256 scale where 0 is black and 256 is white. This range of RGB brightness is defined as follows: The brightest hue of the particular color used for the background, whether it be red, green, or blue, should not be higher than 175 or lower than 155. This RGB range as a background color will be a good base from which a suitable top shadow and bottom shadow color can be derived.

The background color must also provide enough contrast to the foreground color that will be used as the text color on all widget interfaces. If the background color is on the light side, it should provide enough contrast against a black foreground text color. If the background color is on the dark side, it should provide enough contrast against a white foreground text color. Highly saturated colors, such as pure blue, red, or yellow, should be avoided as background colors for a variety of reasons. Any of these as well as other colors of high saturation are harsh on the eyes and are not comfortable to look at for long periods of time. Although Motif's color algorithm does an excellent job in calculating the correct top and bottom shadows, in almost all levels of color brightness and saturation, restrain yourself from using bright saturated colors for best visual results. If bright, saturated background colors are required for special purposes, such as warnings or emergency buttons, Motif's color algorithm will sometimes adjust the hue to achieve the correct top and bottom shadows. Figure 2–3 shows a widget background color and its optimum color range not exceeding 175 on its brightest Red, Green, or Blue color.

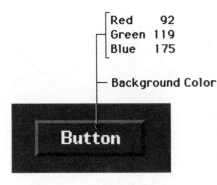

```
⎡ Red      92
⊢ Green   119
⎣ Blue    175
```

⊢ **Background Color**

FIGURE 2–3 The background color's optimum color range should not exceed 175 as its brightest color. The RGB number in this example is a mid-blue color.

Select Color

The select color is a slightly darker variation of the background color. It is not as dark as the bottom shadow color. It is rather about halfway between the background color and the darker bottom shadow color. This color was developed for areas that must show either a momentary selection state, as when a Pushbutton is pressed, or an area where the user is able to edit, such as in an editable Text area. These areas should be filled in with this select color. It can be created by going down the RGB scale a certain percentage and not quite hitting black. We found that approximately 15 percent is an appropriate range to go down the scale of the RGB values. Select color is a resource for buttons, which are set automatically to this slightly darker color. When used in recessed widgets, such as List or Text, it has to be set as the background color. Widgets such as Scale and Scrollbar use the select color in their troughs.

The select color can be calculated by multiplying the background color R,G, and B numbers each by .85 to achieve the select color's R,G, and B numbers. This will result in a slightly darker tint of the background color but not as dark as will be required for the bottom shadow color. Figure 2–4 shows a widget's select color and its approximate calculation from the background color.

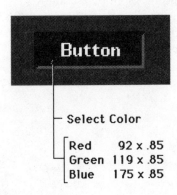

Select Color

Red	92 x .85
Green	119 x .85
Blue	175 x .85

FIGURE 2–4 The select color's approximate value is calculated from the background color. It is approximately 85 percent of the value of the RGB colors of the background color.

Top Shadow

The top shadow is the area that appears to be the light colored chamfer of the widget. Top shadows in widgets that protrude from the background are the top and left chamfers. Top shadows in widgets that recede into the background are the bottom and right chamfers. The top shadow color in every widget is made up of the light-colored chamfers derived from the background color. The light color is created as a variation of the background color. It can be created by going up the RGB scale a certain percentage and not quite hitting white. We found that 40 percent to 50 percent is an appropriate range to go up the scale of the RGB values. This will work very well for mid-valued background colors. For highly saturated colors, the Motif algorithm may at times adjust the hue (the color position in the color wheel) as well as the saturation (the amount of pure color pigment) to get good results. This will prevent results like purple top shadows on a blue background. Because the brightness or luminosity scale is at its peak in a bright color, these other methods must be used to achieve the correct highlight color for the top shadow. If these results are not satisfactory for top and bottom shadows of saturated colors, you might have to decrease the saturation manually and tweak the hue as needed until you achieve satisfactory results. Figure 2–5 shows a widget's top shadow color and its approximate calculation from the background color.

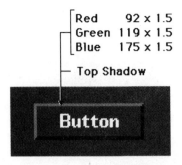

$$\begin{bmatrix} \text{Red} & 92 \times 1.5 \\ \text{Green} & 119 \times 1.5 \\ \text{Blue} & 175 \times 1.5 \end{bmatrix}$$

— Top Shadow

Pushbutton example

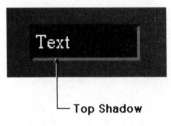

└─ **Top Shadow**

Text Widget example

FIGURE 2–5 The top shadow color's approximate value is calculated from the background color. It is approximately one and a half times the value of the RGB colors of the background color.

The top shadow color can be calculated by multiplying the background color R,G, and B numbers each by 1.50 to achieve the top shadow color's R,G, and B numbers. This will result in a lighter tint of the background color. On certain colors, an adjustment of the hue and saturation will also be necessary to achieve a convincing top shadow color.

Bottom Shadow

The bottom shadow is the darkest colored area that appears to be the dark colored chamfer of the widget. Bottom shadows in widgets that protrude from the background are the bottom and right chamfers. Bottom shadows in widgets that recede into the background are the top and left chamfers. The bottom shadow color is the darkest color derived from the background color. It can be created by going down the RGB scale approximately 45 percent to 60 percent. This provides a good dark color based on the background color without hitting black. The bottom shadow color can be calculated by multiplying the background color R,G, and B numbers each by .50. This will provide the darkest usable tint of the background color. Figure 2–6 shows a widget's bottom shadow color and its approximate calculation from the background color.

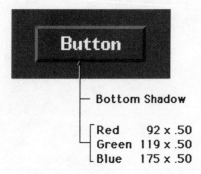

Bottom Shadow

Red   92 x .50
Green   119 x .50
Blue   175 x .50

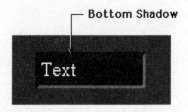

Bottom Shadow

FIGURE 2–6 The bottom shadow color's approximate value is calculated from the background color. It is approximately one half the value of the RG&B colors of the background color.

Foreground Color
The foreground color is a separate color that is not part of the quad of colors that is used as the label or pixmap color in widgets. Motif will determine the correct foreground color automatically depending on the resultant brightness of the R,G, and B values of the background color of the widget. Depending on the background color of the widget, it will flip the foreground color to either black or white.

Traversal Highlight Color
The traversal highlight color is the color assigned to the traversal highlight outline that highlights each widget when it is traversed to by either the keyboard or the mouse. The quad for each widget color does not include the traversal highlight color. The traversal highlighting mechanism is provided by each widget, but its color must be set independently. This same color is used to highlight any widget in a given color scheme.

Color Schemes

A color scheme should be made up of a palette of colors that will impart a mood or a feeling. For instance, "Spring" can contain greens, yellows, or light blues to connote the colors of spring, and "Southwestern" can contain corals, deep purples, teals, and clays to evoke the moods in the southwestern deserts of New Mexico. In creating color schemes from the colors available in your system, use a variety of colors that are different enough to differentiate the interface component areas while still remaining compatible in character with one another. A palette of colors that would comprise a scheme should be used one at a time in an environment and should not be forced to be combined with other color palettes. As a rule, a color scheme should be pervasive throughout the entire screen environment. Should a color scheme be changed to a new one, the colors of all applications on the screen should be affected. A guideline for the use of these color schemes in the design of applications will help ensure predictable results.

Although most color displays can accommodate 256 color spaces, which seems quite abundant, careful application of colors is necessary in order to avoid using up too much of the available color cells. There are times when an application such as a graphics application will demand as many color cells as are available to display an image. A situation like this could eat up most of the color cells and not leave much left over for your applications. Therefore, even if you have an abundant amount of color space available, these cells can be eaten up any time by other applications.

This necessity for quads (the sets of four colors required per widget color) can quickly add up and fill up your color map. For instance, if your application requires 2 colors (2 quads equaling 8 colors) and another application requires 2 different colors, you are already using up 16 colors to satisfy the color quads required by each of the 4 widget colors. Add in the active and inactive window manager colors (6 total because they require only 3 color cells for each state — no select color) as well as black and white (these are always required and count as 2 colors) and the environment background colors (2 if you are using a bitmapped background), you are already up to 26 individual colors. Add to that 2 more applications, each requiring their own 2 quads of color in each of their client areas, and the number of colors adds up to 42 colors. The total number of colors required so far is 42 and we have only 4 applications displayed on the screen. This does not seem like much so far unless you consider that this adds up to 16 percent of a 256 color cell color map and 65 percent of a 64 color cell color map. It won't be long until you use up most of your color map.

A logical strategy for efficient use of color cells will help to minimize the use of available color cells and still keep your application environment visually appealing. One approach to minimizing the use of color cells is by implementing a logical color coding of the application environment. This would go a long way in efficient use of the color map as well as providing enough variety in colors to create a visually rich environment. Where possible, assign the same color to an area that is common throughout all of your applications and use a different color only in an area that will be the most logical for differentiation.

An area that we found to work well for differentiation is the Menubar. The Menubar can be used as the area for color coding. Because all applications should have a Menubar along the top portion of the application's work area, each application can have a different color assigned to it. The rest of the application background, which is the main working area, can share the same color. This eliminates the need to have different colors in every application, and allows you to differentiate with colors only where appropriate. Assigning a different color to each application's Menubar helps to establish several things. Aside from saving color cell space, this technique also adds ergonomic and aesthetic appeal to application windows. It allows the user to identify an application quickly by color association, it allows us to assign a consistent muted pleasing color for the work area in each application window, and because most dialog boxes are spawned from Menu selections, it allows us to color code each dialog box with the same color as its parent application's Menubar. In a multi-windowed environment, this is very useful, because the color helps to indicate where each dialog box comes from. Figure A–6 (color section) shows efficient color space usage by color coding application Menubars.

Gray Scale

Gray scale is the term used to imply that all of the colors that are used to color your application are basically varying shades or brightness of gray. Using gray scale in a color display can greatly conserve the number of color cells used in the color server when the maximum available color is needed for other applications. There are several ways to achieve gray scale in your applications. Techniques designing for gray scale can be used in color displays as well as in monitors that display only shades of gray. The following table shows how many shades of gray can be achieved with varying types of display cards.

Type of Card	Number of Colors or Shades
2-bit	4
4-bit	16
8-bit	256

Let's look at a typical gray scale color scheme and how it will work with Motif. For this example, I will refer to a 2-bit, or 4-color, situation. A typical 2-bit gray scale monitor will display black, white, and 2 levels of gray. This provides us with the ability to create convincing three-dimensional effects without color and the expensive display card required for color. The four shades of gray provide us with the minimum variety of values (brightness levels) to create a convincing three-dimensional look. The following list shows recommended applications of the four gray shades. Figure 2–7 shows widgets in an application with gray scale assigned to it.

Top shadow: White

Panel Background: Light Gray

User Select: Dark Gray

Bottom Shadow: Black

Foreground Text: White

A form of color coding can be achieved by using these four grays also. A designated area such as the Menubar can be used to differentiate one application from another, as in the multicolored scheme. This can be achieved by using the two different shades of gray and also incorporating various dithered patterns to expand the variety of grays.

The use of dithered patterns, also called *texture mapping*, can greatly expand the variety of grays available to you. Dithered patterns fool the eye into believing that the combination of two values are creating a new color altogether. This effect works because the dots displayed by the monitor seem to bloom causing the human eye to average out the two shades of gray. By using the standard 25 percent, 50 percent, and 75 percent dithered patterns, you can expand the number of grays significantly. Figure 2–8 shows various coding possibilities with gray scale using dithered patterns.

Monochrome

On monochrome displays, you are not offered a range of colors. Instead, you have a choice between black or white. Although Motif so far has been explained as color widgets, we cannot ignore the fact that almost half of the marketplace still buys monochrome displays for reasons of cost as well as people's preference. Because eye irritation caused from sensitivity to the display's color alignment, some people are forced to use monochrome displays. This irritation is sometimes due to color monitors employing a shadow mask for aligning colors. This inherently reduces image sharpness, causing some users to have varying levels of sensitivity to less sharp images.

Here is a scheme that will allow Motif's widgets to work visually in monochrome as well as in color. The technique of dithering is recommended to be used here. By dithering black and white in various patterns, you can come up with a variety of shades of gray. We have experimented with

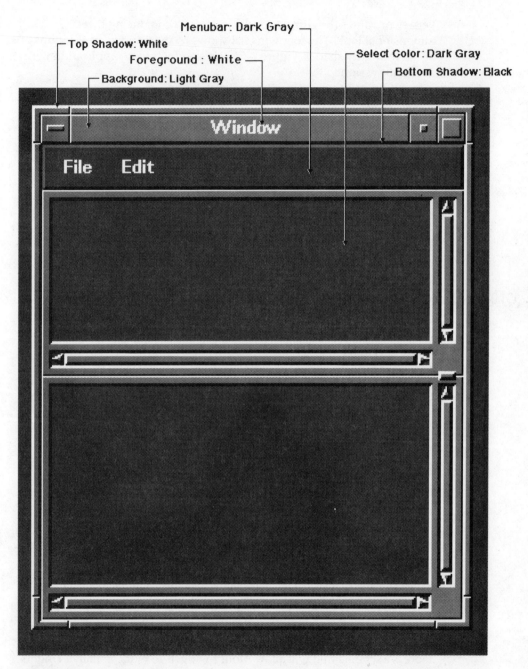

FIGURE 2–7 Gray scale can provide a very compelling appearance to an application without the need to use many colors. Here are the recommended shades of gray to be assigned to an application's widgets.

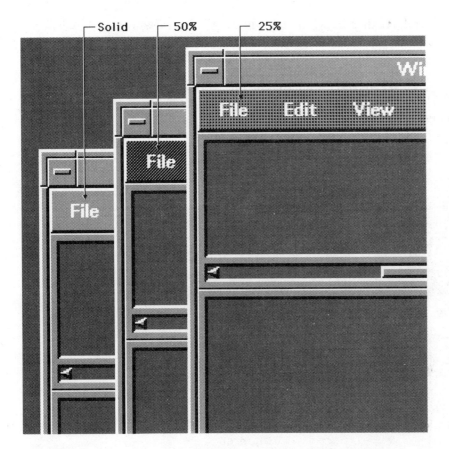

FIGURE 2–8 Color-coding such as that shown in figure A–6 (color section) can be achieved with gray scaling and use of various dithered patterns in each application's Menubar.

25-percent, 50-percent and 75-percent dithered patterns that will result in different shades of gray. This effect is caused by the human eye's natural averaging of dots that appear to bloom when displayed in these patterns. As was mentioned in the section on gray scale, the human eye can be fooled somewhat with the use of dithered patterns. By incorporating varying dithered patterns in black and white, you can easily produce three shades of gray.

Text tends to break up when used with a dithered background. With this in mind, the recommended areas in which to apply a dithered background are areas without text. If text absolutely has to be on a dithered pattern, the text should use double-pixeled or bold fonts, such as the ones recommended for system fonts in chapter 3. Insensitive labels will not show up well on dithered patterns, because Motif assigns a 50-percent dithered pattern to insensitive text. Single-pixeled fonts, such as user fonts, also do not show up well against dithered patterns. Their detail gets lost between the alternating dots and will disappear. Figure 2–9 shows various dithered percentages as well as patterns and how fonts break up against dithered backgrounds.

FIGURE 2–9 Various dithered patterns can be used for area differentiation; however, caution must be excercised if placing fonts against patterns.

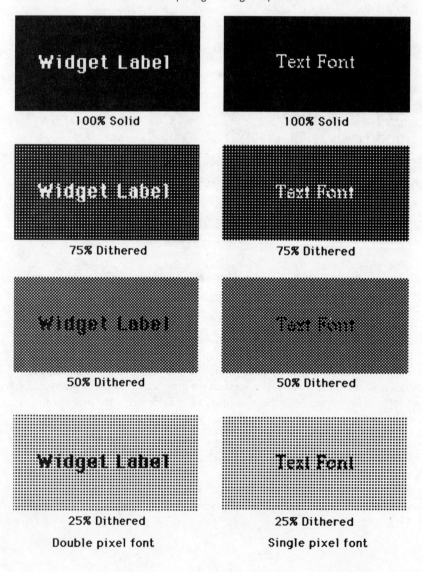

100% Solid	100% Solid
75% Dithered	75% Dithered
50% Dithered	50% Dithered
25% Dithered	25% Dithered
Double pixel font	Single pixel font

By using dithered patterns on the widgets, you will be able to create the illusion of varying gray values. The following lists are recommended applications of the dithered patterns in a monochrome environment.

Black foreground on white background:

Top shadow: 50 percent

Background: White

User Select: Black

Bottom Shadow: Black

Foreground text: Black

Panel Background: White

Figure 2–10 shows a widget (Pushbutton) with assigned areas for dithering in black on white.

Figure 2–11 shows an application using dithered patterns in black on white.

White foreground on black background:

Top shadow: White

Panel Background: Black

User Select: White

Bottom Shadow: 50 percent

Foreground: White

Figure 2–12 shows a widget (Pushbutton) with assigned areas for dithering in white on black.

Figure 2–13 shows an application using dithered patterns in white on black.

Notice in the recommended schemes in figures 2–11 and 2–13 that the select and the bottom shadow colors are recommended to be of the inverted color of the foreground. Motif is designed so that the select color will not bleed into the top shadow. Pushbuttons, Toggles, and Text widgets display a margin around the font cells inside the center when selected. This margin is created automatically and is displayed as a 1-pixel ring around the center label or text area of the widget. This creates a contrasting ring around the selected text, thus separating the select color from the respective top or bottom shadow that it would otherwise bleed into. This feature is enforced automatically by Motif when the select color is specified as the inverse of the foreground color, such as in monochrome, or when the select color is specified as either the top or bottom shadow color. In monochrome, there is no choice other than to use the opposite color for selection. Figure 2–14 shows how the contrast margin surrounding the label in a Pushbutton in monochrome keeps the select color from bleeding into the bottom shadow.

Color coding of key areas can also be done with the use of dithered patterns. For instance, the background shades can be varied by using 25 percent, 50 percent, and 75 percent. Solid black as well as white can also be used; however, the top and bottom shadows would have to be changed if using black or white to the pattern style mentioned earlier in monochrome schemes. Fonts, however, suffer visually against a dithered background. Though I show it in this book, I would not recommend displaying fonts against a dithered background. Figure 2–15 shows various coding possibilities with dithered patterns, such as in the Menubar and other areas. Notice how the fonts tend to break up when displayed against a dithered background.

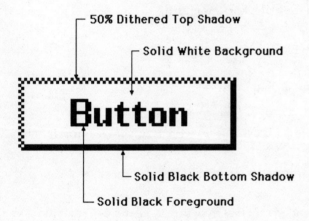

FIGURE 2–10 Black-on-white color schemes can appear three-dimensional if you dither the top shadow and use solid black in the bottom shadow.

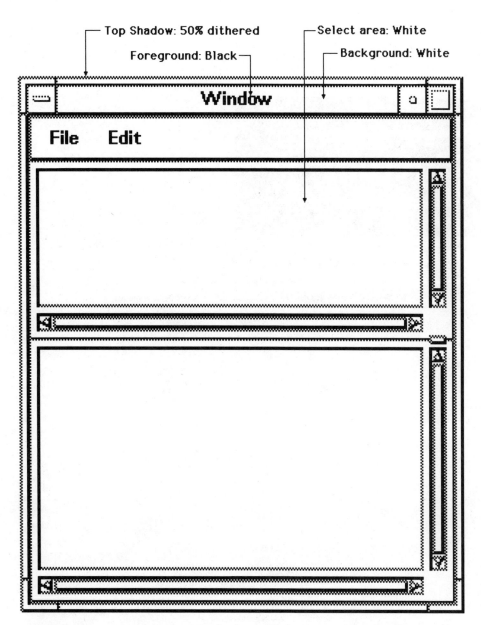

FIGURE 2–11 Black-on-white color schemes in an application can use dithered patterns and solid black to achieve a three-dimensional appearance.

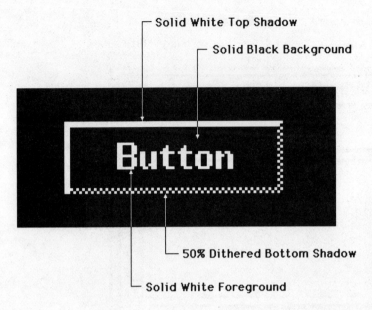

Solid White Top Shadow

Solid Black Background

50% Dithered Bottom Shadow

Solid White Foreground

FIGURE 2–12 White-on-black color schemes can appear three-dimensional if you use solid white in the top shadow and dither the bottom shadow.

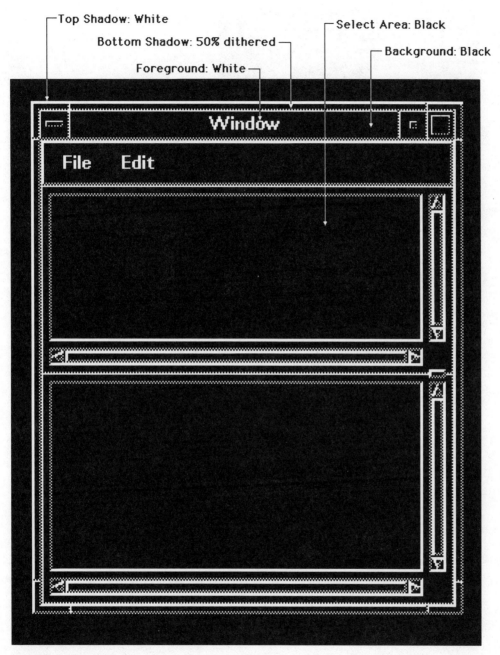

Top Shadow: White

Bottom Shadow: 50% dithered

Foreground: White

Select Area: Black

Background: Black

FIGURE 2–13 White-on-black color schemes in an application can use dithered patterns and solid white to achieve a three-dimensional appearance.

Widget Unselected

Widget Armed

FIGURE 2–14 To prevent the select color from bleeding into the bottom shadow in monochrome widgets, a contrasting outline surrounding the Label in a Pushbutton is employed automatically by Motif.

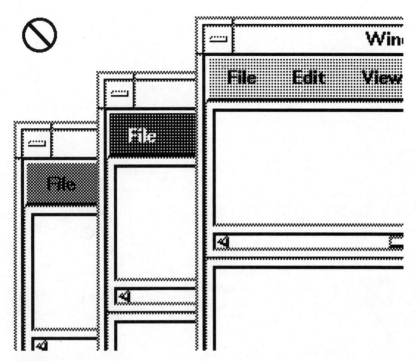

FIGURE 2–15 Dithered patterns should not be used as a differentiating technique in monochrome, because the fonts tend to break up when displayed against a dithered background.

Fonts

Throughout the history of graphical communication, fonts either have played a role or have been an element in setting a mood or attracting attention. No communication design is complete without careful thought about which font to use to deliver the intended message. Successful advertisement has always relied on font styles to attract the correct market audience or to create the desired image for the goods or services it was selling. Fonts can be expressive and whimsical in order to attract attention. For example, movie posters have for years used expressive font styles for attracting attention. Fonts can also be serious and connote no-nonsense text that exudes credibility, such as that in newspapers or books. Subtlety in the size and style of these fonts have a big effect in this case. As an example, the fonts that are selected for a control panel or the dashboard on your car must communicate immediately and without unnecessary fanfare or decoration the status of the operating condition of the vehicle. This information must be trusted by the driver in order for him or her to feel confident in deciding whether to slow down or speed up, deciding whether to pull over because of an overheating engine, or simply confirming that a favorite radio station is tuned in.

The Role of Fonts

In Motif, the application designer can employ both whimsical and serious fonts. Whimsical fonts might help grab the attention of the audience you are developing a document for, and serious, no-nonsense fonts help users find the interface components quickly and effortlessly in your application. This chapter focuses on no-nonsense fonts for use with your application's visual interface. Your application will benefit greatly by your understanding which type of font is appropriate for which application area.

Fonts serve two basic purposes in a graphical user interface. The computer communicates to the user through displayed words, and the user communicates back by creating documents or assigning commands with words. These two points of communication must be comprehensible at all times by the user. We saw an opportunity to further clarify this to the user and differentiate the two types of communication by employing a different font for communications from the system to the user than for communications from the user to the system. We call these two styles *system* and *user* fonts. Unlike in other GUIs, in which the same styled font is used regardless of whether the system is displaying a message or a user is typing into a text area, in Motif, we found it useful to differentiate the two with different font styles.

System Fonts

System fonts are the fonts that are used in the interface components of your application. The use of these fonts should be consistent throughout the entire application. These are the fonts that create the messages as well as the widget labels that users depend on to enable them to use an application with the least amount of surprise and inconsistency. This font should be able to be read easily, with a minimum of decoration or style that would detract from clearly conveying the message. This font should be consistent throughout all of the different widgets that you will need for your application.

System fonts, designed for the user interface, are straightforward and nonobtrusive in character. We designed an HP proprietary sans serif font in various sizes for use as the system interface font. The look and legibility of your application's interface design is greatly affected by which font you select or design for your application. Legibility and clarity were key design guidelines in the selection of which type of font to use in the interface of an application. Sans serif fonts work the best in conveying a refined and purposeful look to Motif. Serif fonts, though fine for the long sentences of books and other printed materials, do not look as clean or as easy to read in the few words on widgets. Sans serif fonts tend to be more legible and purposeful than serif fonts. The selection of sans serif fonts for use in the system interface is also consistent with the style of fonts used in interface components of other GUIs. Figure 3–1 shows a comparison between serif and sans serif fonts.

The font that is used in your application should be consistent in style and size and should also be legible across different display resolution densities. Different font sizes within an application are not recommended for reasons of inconsistency in widget spacing and legibility. By keeping the font consistent throughout your application, you will also be assured of the correct alignment of widgets, because all widgets are sized according to the font within them. The character stroke width of the system font should be at least 2 pixels in thickness. This provides good legibility when system fonts are displayed as insensitive by the system. When displayed as insensitive, characters appear in a 50 percent dithered (checkered) pattern. The selected font style should be legible in various display resolutions from 72 ppi (pixels per inch) to 120 ppi.

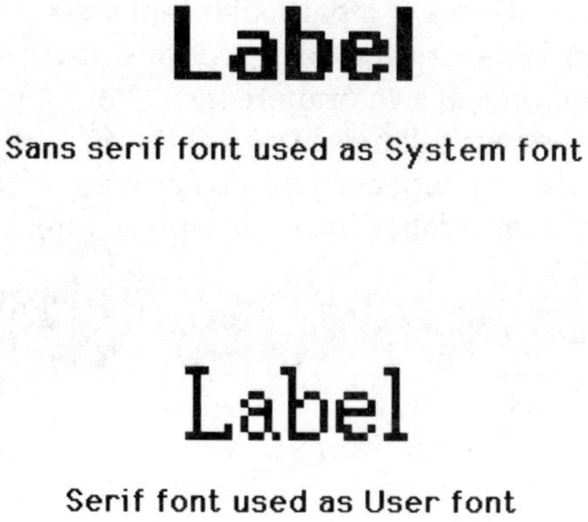

Label

FIGURE 3–1 Comparison of serif and sans serif fonts.

Sans serif font used as System font

Label

Serif font used as User font

The following recaps what system fonts are not:

- System fonts are not WYSIWYG (what you see is what you get) fonts.
- They are not fonts that you can print out from what you see on the screen.
- They are not fonts that are derived from an outline.
- They are not fonts that print out in a graphics application.
- They are not fonts whose character you can change dynamically from Times Roman to Palatino.
- They are not fonts that you use for desktop publishing or for graphic design.

System fonts are bitmapped fonts specifically designed for labeling your widgets and for displaying system messages. Figure 3–2 shows various styles of fonts that would not be appropriate as system fonts.

System fonts are specifically designed bitmapped fonts represented by what are called *glyphs* consistently positioned within their character cell. Glyphs are the bitmapped patterns in a font cell that characterize a style and size of a font character. These characters will work predictably with widgets. System fonts can be laid out to be fixed pitch or variable pitch. For widget labeling, variable pitch fonts are recommended because of their legibility and space efficiency. Figure 3–3 shows the type of font that would be appropriate as a system font with its glyphs positioned correctly.

System fonts are special, because they must work in a variety of situations. The rules governing these fonts must also be used when words are translated to another language. For instance, these fonts must work in German as well as in English. They must be designed for the use of diacritical marks as well, which means that extra space in the character cell must be designed for diacritics from the beginning.

An interface will usually contain several sizes of a particular font style. Such a set containing different sized fonts must be designed for consistency. For instance, a set can contain fonts of two or more sizes. You can vary widget size just by increasing the font cell height by as little as one pixel, because the relative width of the font cell will also grow. Figure 3–4 shows a comparison of the same label with a one-pixel difference in height between them.

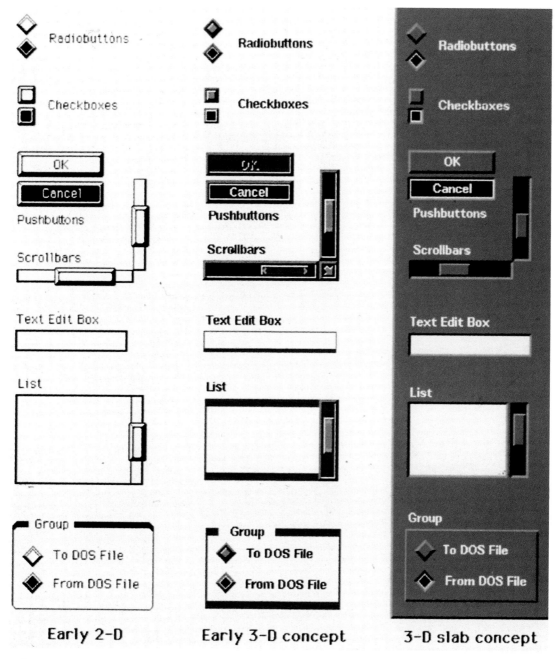

FIGURE A–I The three-dimensional visual design of Motif evolved over a few months from a flat two-dimensional appearance (left) into a complex three-dimensional look that required approximately eight shades of gray (center). The final design (right) was simplified to enable better performance, and it established the slablike appearance.

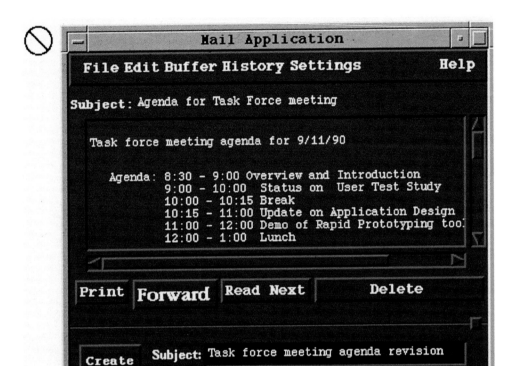

FIGURE A–2 This is an example of a poorly configured visual application interface. Details such as inconsistent use of fonts, overly generous spacing between widgets, misalignment of widgets, and general lack of visual attention to color and visual proportions contribute to an awkwardly appearing application.

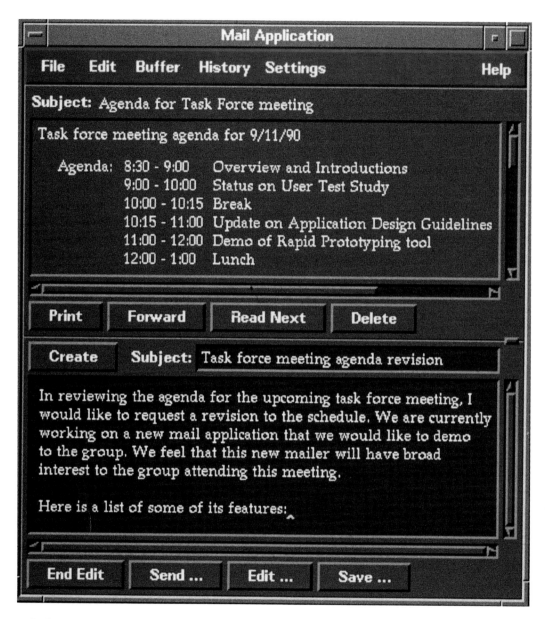

FIGURE A–3 This is an example of a properly designed application interface. Attention was paid to the finest details such as font consistency, minimal spacing, widget alignment, and proportional widget sizing as well as to sensitivity to color harmony. These all contribute to an application's visual quality.

Do not use saturated colors for widgets.

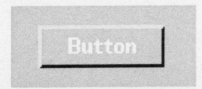

Do not use borderline colors that mistakenly calculate the wrong foreground color.

Do not overwrite the calculated top and bottom shadows with other colors.

Do not assign patterns to the background color of widgets.

FIGURE A–4 This is an example of how widgets are affected by colors and patterns. Exercise restraint when assigning colors to your widgets.

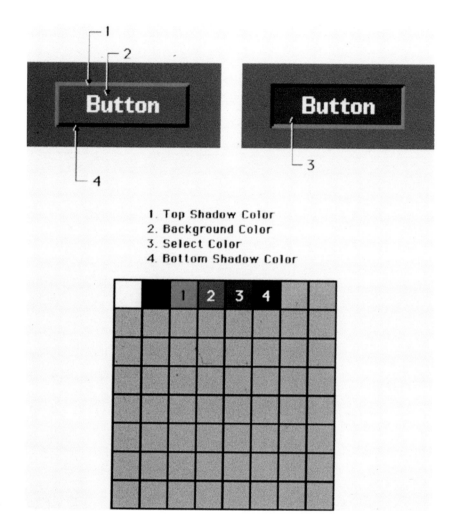

FIGURE A–5 Every color assigned to a widget requires four color spaces from the color map. If colors are not efficiently used, color spaces can be taken up very quickly.

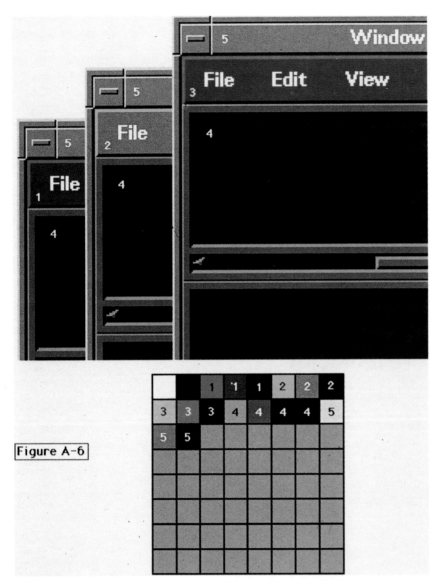

Figure A-6

FIGURE A-6 Color coding by assigning different colors to each applications's Menubar can help differentiate each application while not utilizing too many color spaces. This also creates a tasteful visual quality to your suite of applications.

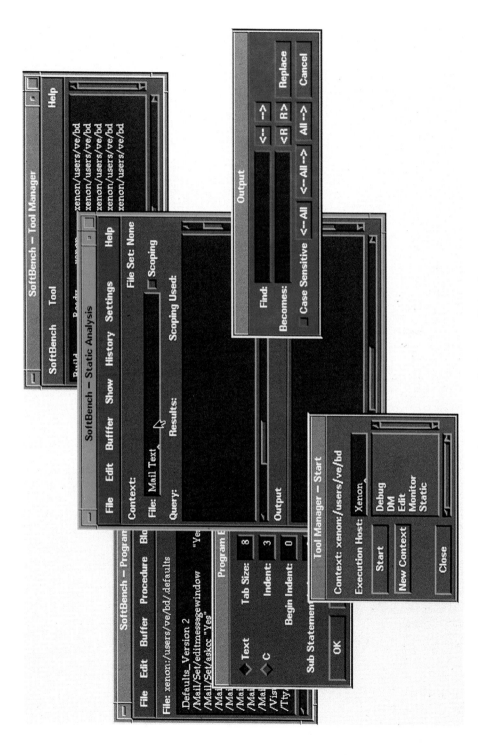

FIGURE A–7 In a multiwindowed screen environment where many applications are displayed at once, color coding can help the user identify each application and tell at a glance from where each dialog box appeared.

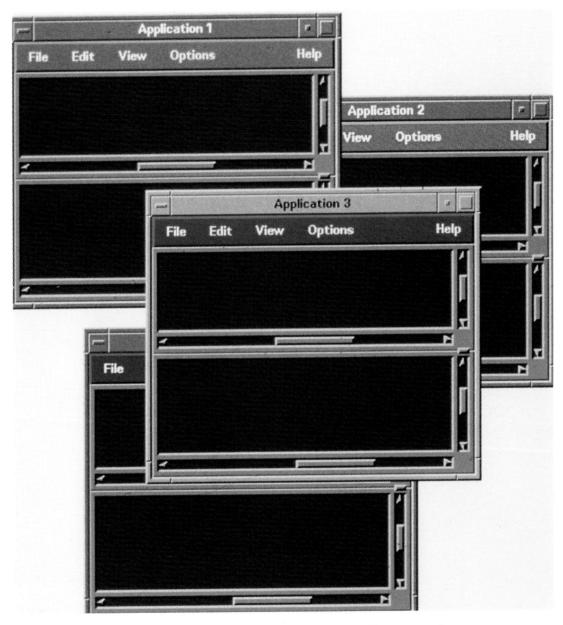

FIGURE A-8 The bright active window should be assigned a color that is bright or saturated enough to be easily noticed while harmonizing with the overall color scheme of the screen environment.

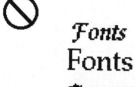

Fonts
Fonts
𝕱𝖔𝖓𝖙𝖘
𝑭𝒐𝒏𝒕𝒔

FIGURE 3–2 Examples of various styles of fonts that would not be appropriate as system fonts.

FIGURE 3–3 Glyphs in a font cell provide the visual character of a font. They are positioned consistently in each font cell for predictable layout when used as Labels.

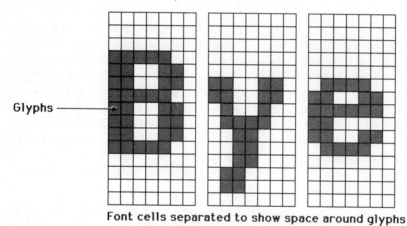

Glyphs

Font cells separated to show space around glyphs

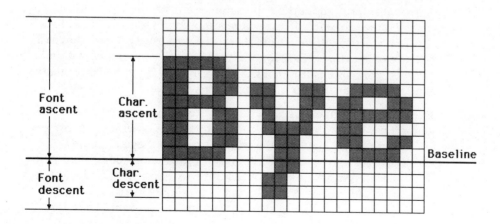

Font ascent

Char. ascent

Font descent

Char. descent

Baseline

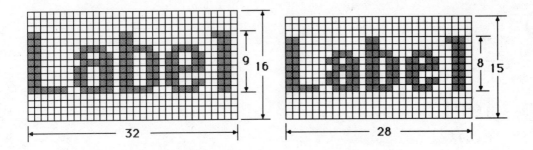

9 pixel high character in   8 pixel high character in
a 16 pixel high font cell.   a 15 pixel high font cell.

FIGURE 3–4 A one-pixel difference in height within a font set also affects the length of the Label, because its width is also proportional to the font's height.

The glyphs in the font cell should be positioned so that they line up predictably with other letters of the font family. The amount of ascent and descent of their glyphs must be consistent per font size. The font cells as well should be consistent in height when pairing up different styles of fonts. Although the X window system provides the capability of aligning fonts on their respective baselines, Motif forces fonts contained within widgets to ignore this. All widgets are registered from their upper-left corner and as a result all fonts contained within them must be aligned manually by specifying their margin heights. Figure 3–5 shows a comparison of how a one-pixel difference in font height can misalign dissimilar widgets.

Though it is tempting to use a dazzling array of fonts and sizes in a program, show good taste through your restraint. Use the same font for similar widgets throughout the application. For instance, all Labels should use the same font and all Text widgets should use the same font. Labels and Text will use different fonts, because Label uses a system font and Text uses a user font. These fonts should be used consistently within each widget type. This ensures that the letters in all widgets are aligned horizontally and that all interface components are equally readable.

To help you design or specify a font for use in a widget, let's take a closer look at how fonts affect the look and proportions of widgets. Fonts govern the width and height of the widget in which they are located. All widgets are designed to have their resources or dimensions set from the height and the width of the font cells. The margin height and width in a Pushbutton, for instance, are defined as pixel dimensions from the font cell. This dimension should also grow when a larger font size is used.

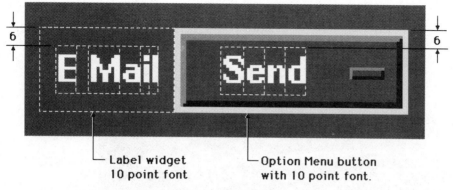

6 ↕   6 ↕

└─ Label widget   └─ Option Menu button
   10 point font   with 10 point font.

Label & Option Menu button aligned correctly

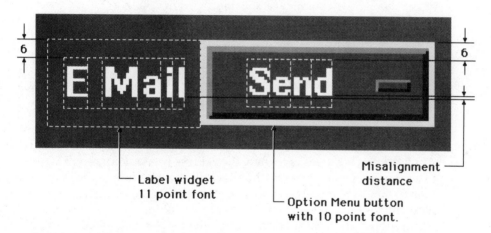

6 ↕   6 ↕

                                    Misalignment ─────
                                    distance

└─ Label widget   └─ Option Menu button
   11 point font   with 10 point font.

FIGURE 3–5 Misalignment in dissimilar widgets can occur as a result of fonts whose heights are off by as little as one pixel.

This makes it even more important that various font heights of a particular interface font not be used in widgets. Figure 3–6 shows how using varying font sizes can greatly affect the alignment of like widgets.

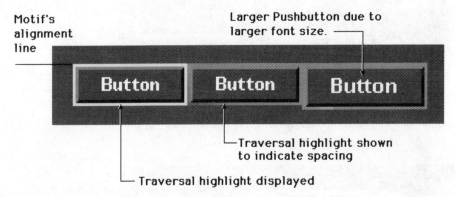

Motif's alignment line

Larger Pushbutton due to larger font size.

Traversal highlight shown to indicate spacing

Traversal highlight displayed

FIGURE 3–6 Fonts of different heights will affect the height and the alignment of similar widgets when placed together. Fonts of larger size also require extra margin height for visual balance. This will also accentuate the misalignment.

User Fonts

Application work areas are where the expressive use of fonts will take place. This is where users may be allowed to select a font of their choice or may simply be presented with a font style that is different from the system font. Free expression of a variety of fonts is fine for creative documents; however, there are many times when a user is required to enter information where fonts of less expressive style are more appropriate. Such fonts are often used in applications in which the user must type in a name, address, passwords, or file names. They also often are used in areas that require one or a few lines of text entry, usually accompanied by a Label or a brief message indicating the type of information required. Such user or edit areas, where the user is responsible for inputting information requested by the system or information that will send a command to the system, are called *user areas.* User fonts are those we implement in user areas.

User areas called for a differentiator in font style that would help reinforce to the user the difference between system-displayed information and user-entered information. We have found that most users prefer using serif fonts like Courier in such areas. From this research, we designed an HP proprietary font set specifically designed to be paired up with our system fonts. This user font, when used with its specific system font, provides a matched set that communicates to the user when the system is displaying a message and when the user can enter or edit information.

The design of an application will benefit from the use of user and system font styles. Along with the use of select color areas, such use will help reinforce the differentiation between system area and user area.

When choosing or developing user fonts, you should always pair them with system fonts. User font cells should be the same height as the system fonts that will be used with them. The glyphs within the character cell for a user font should be positioned at the same location and have the same height as those for the associated system font. Figure 3–7 shows system fonts with user fonts lined up together.

FIGURE 3–7 System fonts are often lined up with user fonts in the design of interfaces. Attention to font height and top and bottom spacing will assure consistent alignment.

Widgets

4

Chapter

The OSF/Motif widgets are a set of graphical user interface components that implement the OSF/Motif Style Guide behavior. This is based on user interface behavioral standards established in IBM's (International Business Machine's) CUA (Common User Access) and Presentation Manager user specifications. These basic widgets and the tasks that they perform fulfill the majority of the range of functions required by almost any application's interface. OSF/Motif's basic widget set forms the foundation of any application that will be written using Motif as its graphical user interface.

Widgets are the interface components that allow the user to manipulate applications without having to use often complex and hard-to-remember sequences of text input. Widgets are like self-contained modules of code that perform a variety of tasks by means of consistent operation by the user. Some widgets perform simple tasks, such as a Toggle, which only has to tell the system to turn something on or off. Some of the Motif widgets handle more complex functions, such as Scrolled Windows, which must determine a whole set of operations that would allow it to scroll one line at a time, to select an area, or to jump from area to area in many directions.

Primitive and Manager Widgets

Motif's widgets are designed in a hierarchical system and are classified as primitive and manager widgets. Primitive widgets are widgets that cannot contain any other widget in them. Manager widgets are widgets that can have within them other primitive and manager widgets. Widgets such as Pushbuttons and Labels are examples of primitive widgets. They cannot contain within them another widget of the same or different function. These primitive widgets are often grouped with other primitive widgets in a manager widget. Primitive widgets cannot be manager widgets.

Primitive widgets are as follows:

- Label
- Pushbutton
- Toggle
- Arrow
- Separator
- Cascade Button

An example of a primitive widget would be a Pushbutton. As a primitive widget, a Pushbutton cannot contain any other widget within it, nor can it be combined with another widget without losing its identity as a single Pushbutton. Figure 4–1 shows a Pushbutton widget. A Pushbutton is predetermined to do only one function.

Manager widgets are often referred to as parent widgets in an application's hierarchical structure, because they can contain within them other primitive and/or manager widgets. When they are referred to as a parent widget, they must have responsibility as a parent of another widget. Parent widgets can also be children of other parent or manager widgets. This means that they can have within them a child or a set of children widgets while also being child widgets of another parent (manager) widget.

A Frame or a Scrolled Window is an example of a manager widget. A Frame's function is to display itself; it also can contain one child widget. A Scrolled Window is an example of a manager widget formed from a combination of children widgets, which provides the functionality of a window whose contents can be scrolled.

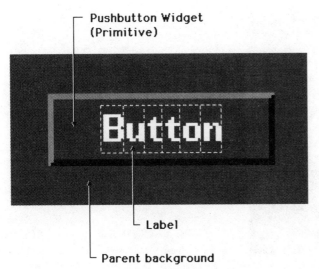

Pushbutton Widget
(Primitive)

Label

Parent background

FIGURE 4–1 A Pushbutton cannot hold within it any other widget. Its function is predetermined
and involves only one action.

Let's look at an example of a container displaying its children. A Frame
widget is used to display printing output choices. One is labeled "Por-
trait," indicating a vertical orientation, and the other is labeled "Land-
scape," indicating a horizontal orientation. Each choice is represented by
a Radiobutton. The Frame is the parent of a Radiobox manager widget,
which is the parent of the two Radiobuttons. The Frame widget, while displaying all of this together, is also a child of another manager widget
that has responsibility of laying out the Frame along with other manager
and primitive widgets. Figure 4–2 shows a Frame with its children and
its parent widget.

What Are Gadgets?

Motif provides *gadgets*, which are widgets stripped of some features in
order to gain higher performance. Gadgets are windowless widgets. The
visual design implications of being a windowless widget results in widgets that cannot have their own independent color assigned to them.
Gadgets are forced to have the same color as their parent widget's color.
They are essentially high-performance widgets without the X window
system overhead necessary in a widget. Currently, six widgets are offered
as gadgets. These are the same as the primitive widgets:

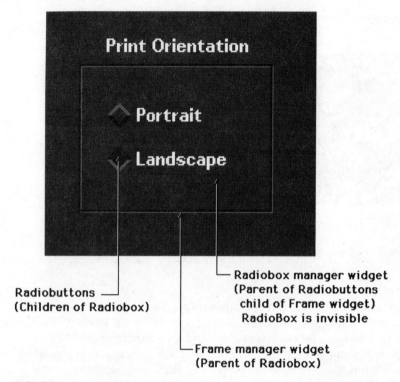

FIGURE 4–2 A Frame is a container widget that can hold one child. In this example its child (a Radiobox widget) holds within it other children (Radiobuttons).

- Label
- Pushbutton
- Toggle
- Arrow
- Separator
- Cascade Button

Let's look at an example of a gadget. For example, if a Pushbutton widget is on a parent background that is blue, the Pushbutton widget can be set to red or yellow if the application designer or the user so desires. A gadget, however, must adopt its parent window's background color. Gadgets hence do not provide a resource for specifying background color. Because Motif-compliant behavior and good design practice recommends that widgets be of the same color as their parent window anyway, the use of gadgets is fine for gaining efficiency and faster performance.

Traversal Highlight

Every widget mentioned in this chapter is incorporated with a highlight-ing mechanism called the *traversal highlight.* This allows each widget to be highlighted one at a time. This indication allows the user to traverse through selections when using the keyboard while providing a visual cue to the current location of the keyboard input focus for keyboard tra-versal. The traversal highlight will also indicate selection with the mouse. The keyboard will then recognize the new position.

The traversal highlight thickness can be specified individually for each widget; however, I recommend setting the same thickness for all widgets. The Motif widgets are designed in such a way that if the traversal high-light thickness is consistent, you will be assured that all of your widgets will line up predictably in your application or dialog box. By default, the thickness of traversal highlight is set to 2 pixels. This can be changed in the traversal highlight thickness resource **XmNtraversalThickness.** I rec-ommend that you do not change this setting, because 2 pixels accom-plishes several things. It creates an aesthetically proportional outline thickness against widgets and provides the minimum amount of spacing between widgets without your having to space widgets apart.

The traversal highlight thickness of every widget in your application should be determined early in the design of your application and should remain consistent throughout the application. Because all positioning of widgets is determined by the outermost element of the widget, the tra-versal thickness is a key element in each widget for layout predictabil-ity. Once the traversal thickness is determined, the widgets can be positioned predictably whether or not you decide to turn the traversal highlight on. The area that is the thickness of the traversal highlight will be held by the widget and will appear to be invisible, showing just its par-ent background color. If it is set to appear when the user traverses to it, the color that is designated as the traversal highlight color will appear as an outline around the widget when the user traverses to it by the mouse or keyboard. Figures B–2 and B–3 (color section) show widgets with their traversal highlights on.

The color of the traversal highlight is determined by the application de-signer. The color should match well with the overall color scheme but be bright enough to stand out from the background. Highlight color can be specified in the resource **XmNhighlightColor.**

The following sections of this chapter will deal with the resource settings of each of OSF Motif's widgets that affect their visual display and layout. These sections are to be used as a guide to visual descriptions of each widget. The illustrative description of each of these widgets will help in the design of visually pleasing and predictable widget proportions.

Resource terminology will be used in the sections that are about to follow. All of the resource settings use the prefix **XmN** or **Xm** and refer to the resource settings that are in the *OSF Motif Programmer's Reference Manual.* An **XmN** prefix indicates a resource specification that has to be set. An **Xm** prefix indicates a setting or pixel value for a particular resource specification. This section will refer only to visual design specifications and not to the technical aspect or event handling of widgets.

The visual examples that are used in this chapter use font cells that are 16 pixels in height with 9-pixel high characters within, as well as the following widget component values:

Traversal Highlight: 2

Shadow Thickness: 2

Margin Height: 2

Margin Width: Specified per widget

Scrolled Window margin height: 2 unless specified

Labels

A Label is a primitive widget typically used to display a string. It is constructed from the font character cells used to create the word. Labels can also contain pixmap images; however, both fonts and pixmaps cannot be contained in the same Label. The text in a Label can be multidirectional, multiline, and or multifont. A Label is represented visually as a word or a string of words colored with a foreground color against a background color. This widget, like many others, has adjustable margin height and width as well as all of the surrounding specifiable margins. This allows Labels to be placed accurately in line with other components. The text of an active or sensitive Label is solid and not dithered. The text for any Label in an application should use a system font. As mentioned in chapter 3, "Fonts," system fonts are at least two pixels in thickness and are proportionally pitched as well as sans serif in visual style. An insensitive Label automatically will be assigned text that is dithered with a 50-percent pattern. By using a two-pixel-width system font, you can achieve dithering that provides good legibility while displaying insensitivity. Figure 4–3 shows sensitive and insensitive Labels.

Typical Label

Insensitive Label

FIGURE 4–3 Sensitive and insensitive Labels. Insensitive Labels
are displayed as 50-percent dithered.

A Label's size is determined by the size of the font character cells that
are within its borders. Along with the size of the font used, a Label's margin height and margin width also help determine its overall widget size.
When a different-sized font replaces the current font in a Label, the margin height and margin width remain the same until changed. This could
cause the Label to appear misaligned with other widgets unless their fonts
are changed also to match the Label's new font size. The differences dictated by varying font sizes will also affect any widgets that use labels, such
as Pushbuttons and Toggles.

Label's margins are specified in the resources **XmNmarginHeight** (margin
height) and **XmNmarginWidth** (margin width). These will center Label's string (text) from top to bottom and from side to side. The following
list describes which margins can be set in a Label:

XmNmarginHeight   This resource setting will specify the
distance in pixels between the top
edge of the top margin and the top
edge of the Label's border. This pixel
value will also specify the distance between the bottom edge of the bottom margin and the lower edge of the
Label's border. Both of these distances will be set simultaneously.

XmNmarginWidth

This resource setting will specify the distance in pixels between the left edge of the left margin and the left edge of the Label's border. This pixel value will also specify the distance between the right edge of the right margin and the right edge of the Label's border. Both of these distances will be set simultaneously.

A Label must be configured so that its text is aligned with other widgets. Because Labels do not use traversal highlights, their outermost top and bottom edge dimensions must equal any accompanying widgets' complete height, including their traversal highlight thickness, for proper horizontal alignment. This can be specified in the resource **XmNmarginHeight,** which defaults to 2 pixels and which should be increased to 6 pixels if it is to be aligned with other widgets, such as a Text widget. This would take into account a Text widget's 2-pixel margin height, 2-pixel top or bottom shadow, and its 2-pixel traversal highlight. Figure 4–4 shows a Label and its visual layout components.

FIGURE 4–4 A Label's visual layout components.

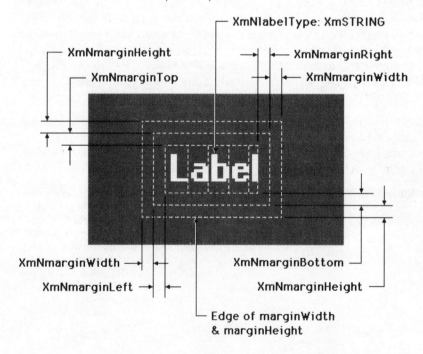

A Label's horizontal spacing will be affected by the length of the text within it. It is a good rule of thumb to allow some space on each side of the Label as well. The Label's resource **XmNmarginWidth** defaults to 2 and should not be changed unless the Label itself requires a change in width.

Labels can also be specified to position their strings other than in the center. In this case, you will have to specify the other margins. These other margins are top margin, **XmNmarginTop,** bottom margin, **XmNmarginBottom,** left margin, **XmNmarginLeft,** and the right margin, **XmNmarginRight.** These will set each margin distance separately from the respective edge of the text and the corresponding edge of Label's margin height or margin width. These margin settings can be used instead of margin height and width as well. This is done by setting **XmNmarginHeight** and **XmNmarginWidth** both to 0. These margins can also be used in conjunction with margin height and width.

XmNmarginTop	This resource setting will specify the distance in pixels between the top side of the text font cell or pixmap and the bottom edge of the upper margin height.
XmNmarginBottom	This resource setting will specify the distance in pixels between the bottom side of the text font cell or pixmap and the top edge of the lower margin height.
XmNmarginLeft	This resource setting will specify the distance in pixels between the left side of the text font cells or pixmap and the right edge of the left margin width.
XmNmarginRight	This resource setting will specify the distance in pixels between the right side of the text font cells or pixmap and the left edge of the right margin width.

I would not recommend using these four margin resources too often unless your application requires some unusual alignment of the Label to some other widget. I would stick to the simple method of specifying margin heights and widths. Figure 4–5 shows a Label's text position when altered with different margin specifications.

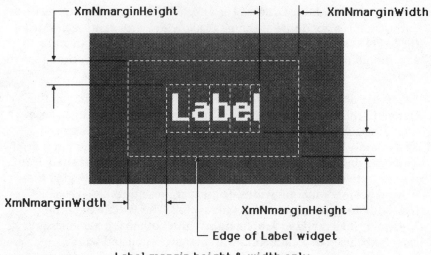

Label margin height & width only

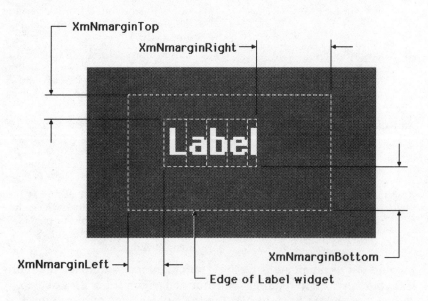

Label top, bottom, left, & right margins only

FIGURE 4–5 A Label's text position is altered when different margins are specified.

Labels often are used to identify other widgets. For example, a Text widget is typically labeled with a few words describing what should go in it. In cases like this, when a Label is set beside or above another widget, you will have to specify the correct margin distances in the Label so that it's string will line up with the text in other widgets.

There are times when a Label will be used where horizontal alignment is visually important. These could be situations where Labels might be stacked, or paired up with other widgets. You might even want to use a Label's orientation to impart a style to your interface. To accommodate this, Label's text or pixmap can be aligned three ways. The text (string) can appear as aligned to the left, centered, or aligned to the right. This text alignment can be specified in the resource **XmNalignment.** The following will describe each alignment specification.

XmALIGNMENT_CENTER   This resource setting will center the line of text or pixmap horizontally across the widget.

XmALIGNMENT_END   This resource setting will align the right side of the line of text or pixmap vertically with the right edge of the widget.

XmALIGNMENT_BEGINNING   This resource setting will align the left side of the line of text or pixmap with the left side of the widget.

Text alignment can vary depending on the situation in which the Label is applied. Labels that are stacked as a list can vary in length, resulting in unpredictable text widths. I suggest that vertically stacked Labels, as well as Labels that are associated with widgets to their left be specified as **XmALIGNMENT_BEGINNING.** This will result in Labels aligned on their left side or aligned to the right of an accompanying widget.

Labels positioned with other widgets to their right should be specified as **XmALIGNMENT_END.** This will result in Labels aligned on the right side. When vertically stacked, they will appear to be aligned on the right side of their column. When these Labels are associated with other widgets and stacked, a center alignment between Labels and their associated widgetswill be created. This type of alignment will prevent the large gaps between Labels and their associated widgets that can occur when they are aligned to the beginning or center. Figure 4–6 shows recommended alignment styles for text Labels when accompanied by another widget to their right.

Labels as a list aligned as
XmALIGNMENT_BEGINNING

Labels associated with other widgets
aligned as XmALIGNMENT_END

FIGURE 4-6 Labels should be left-justified when vertically stacked. When stacked with accompanying widgets such as Text widgets, they should be right-justified so that they will create a center alignment with the Text widgets.

Pixmap alignment can be visually unpredictable and can appear awkward if right or left alignment is used. I recommend using **XmALIGNMENT_CENTER** for aligning pixmaps. Because their visual character can vary in all directions from pixmap to pixmap, there is no predictable visual cue that would allow them to be aligned visually. Unless pixmaps are designed to be visually uniform and to allow some continuity in alignment to the right or left, center alignment works best. Figure 4-7 shows recommended alignment styles for pixmaps.

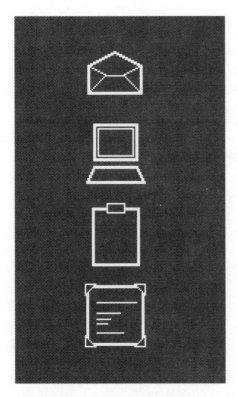

Pixmaps should be aligned as
XmALIGNMENT_CENTER

FIGURE 4–7 Pixmaps should
be center-aligned when stacked.
This allows pixmaps with odd
shapes to appear orderly.

Pushbuttons

Pushbuttons are primitive widgets commonly used to run the same action every time they are pressed with the mouse. They can be used, for example, to invoke or cancel an operation as well as to spawn dialog boxes. Pushbuttons are dynamic buttons that are activated by pressing on them with the mouse pointer. They appear to spring back to their unselected state once the mouse button is released, at which time their action is triggered.

Pushbuttons assign their background color as the flat area on the top. Top shadow color is assigned to the left and top chamfers, and bottom shadow color is assigned to the bottom and right chamfers when the

Pushbutton is displayed in its unselected state. These colors are reversed when the Pushbutton is selected. When selected, its center is assigned its select color. Figure 4–8 shows Pushbuttons as unselected, selected, and insensitive.

Pushbuttons are represented visually as rectangular frames surrounding a Label in their center. When pushed, the Pushbutton's top and bottom shadows reverse and the center changes its color to the select color to emphasize the illusion that it is depressing into the panel background surface. This darker select color indicates the armed state and is activated in the resource **XmNfillOnArm.**

A Pushbutton's size is determined by the size of the font character cells that are within its borders. The margin height and margin width surrounding all sides of a Pushbutton's Label also determines the size of the

FIGURE 4–8 Pushbuttons shown in their unselected, armed, and insensitive states.

Pushbutton Unselected

Pushbutton Armed

Pushbutton Insensitive

Pushbutton. When a new sized font replaces the current font in a Pushbutton, the margin height and margin width will remain the same. This could cause the Pushbutton's Label to appear misaligned with other widgets, unless their fonts were changed also to match the Pushbutton's new font size.

A Pushbutton's margins are specified in the resources **XmNmarginHeight** (margin height) and **XmNmarginWidth** (margin width). These resources will center Pushbutton's Label from top to bottom and from side to side. The following list describes the effect of these resources:

XmNmarginHeight	This resource setting will specify the distance in pixels between the top edge of the top margin and the inside edge of the Pushbutton's top shadow. This pixel value will also specify the distance between the bottom edge of the bottom margin and the inside edge of the Pushbutton's bottom shadow. Both of these distances will be set simultaneously.
XmNmarginWidth	This resource setting will specify the distance in pixels between the left edge of the left margin and the left inside edge of the Pushbutton's top shadow. This pixel value will also specify the distance between the right edge of the right margin and the right inside edge of the Pushbutton's bottom shadow. Both of these distances will be set simultaneously.

XmNmarginHeight defaults to 2 pixels and should remain unchanged for best visual results. **XmNmarginWidth** also defaults to 2 pixels but should be changed to a larger value. A margin width of 2 pixels positions the left and right beveled edges too close to the Pushbutton's Label. You should design in some visual space between the Pushbutton's Label and its left and right edges. A margin width pixel value of 8 would be visually preferable. When you specify horizontal margins with **XmNmarginWidth,** this will also ensure that the Label in Pushbuttons will always be centered. Figure 4–9 shows a Pushbutton's visual layout components.

Pushbuttons can also be specified to position their Labels other than in the center. In this case, you will have to specify the other margins. These other margins are set through **XmNmarginTop** (top margin), **XmNmarginBottom** (bottom margin), **XmNmarginLeft** (left margin),

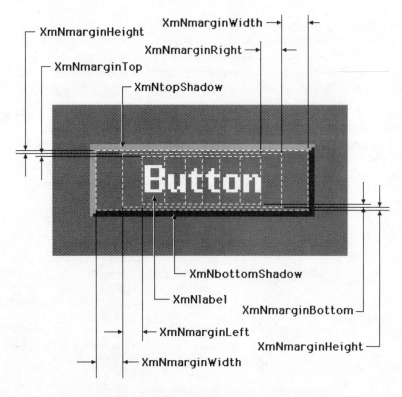

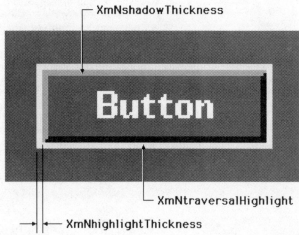

FIGURE 4–9 A Pushbutton's visual layout components.

and **XmNmarginRight** (right margin). These will set each margin distance separately from the respective edge of the text and the corresponding edge of Pushbutton's margin height or margin width. These margin settings can be used in conjunction with or instead of margin height and width. If you choose to use them instead of margin height and width, you must set **XmNmarginHeight** and **XmNmarginWidth** both to 0. The following list describes the effect of each of these resources:

XmNmarginTop	This resource setting will set the distance in pixels between the top side of the text font cells and the bottom edge of the upper margin height.
XmNmarginBottom	This resource setting will set the distance in pixels between the bottom side of the text font cells and the top edge of the lower margin height.
XmNmarginLeft	This resource setting will set the distance in pixels between the left side of the text font cells and the right edge of the left margin width.
XmNmarginRight	This resource setting will set the distance in pixels between the right side of the text font cells and the left edge of the right margin width.

I would not recommend using these four margin resources too often unless your application requires some unusual alignment of the Pushbutton to some other widget. I would stick to the simple method of specifying margin heights and widths. Figure 4–10 shows the varying text positioning available by specifying different margins.

When used in applications, Pushbuttons should be aligned horizontally in rows for space efficiency. When placed in a row, each Pushbutton should display a consistent height, while allowing their individual widths to vary. Any inconsistency in the margin heights between Pushbuttons will cause their Labels to look misaligned as well as causing the Pushbuttons to display different overall heights. When Pushbuttons are placed in a vertical column, the RowColumn manager will force each Pushbutton to the width of the widest Pushbutton, therefore displaying vertically aligned Pushbuttons with the same height and width. Figure 4–11 shows inconsistency in the margin height of a row of Pushbuttons.

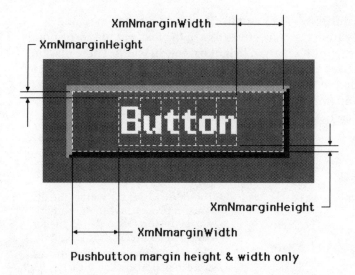

Pushbutton margin height & width only

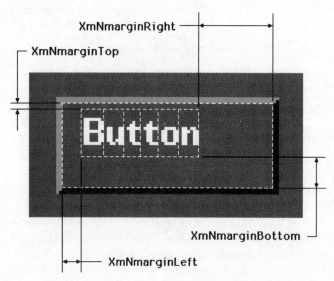

Pushbutton margin top, bottom, left, & right

FIGURE 4–10 A Pushbutton's text positioning is altered when different margins are specified.

FIGURE 4–11 Inconsistency in the margin heights of a row of Pushbuttons causes the Pushbuttons to be of different heights, resulting also in misaligned Labels.

Default Pushbuttons

Default Pushbuttons are used only in Dialog Boxes. The keyboard keys designated to activate the Default Pushbutton are usually Return or Enter. Default Pushbuttons are typically used to confirm and invoke a set of settings that are changed in a Dialog Box. These Pushbuttons are called default because they are labeled with the most likely command that most users will select for invoking a set of changes made in a particular dialog box. This action, when selected by mouse or by keyboard, should also be set to unpost the Dialog Box immediately after invoking the command.

The Default Pushbutton, like the Pushbutton, will be invoked only if the cursor is inside of the Default Pushbutton area at the time of activation with the mouse. This ensures a behavior that will allow users to change their minds during the course of the selection. When invoking a Default Pushbutton through a keyboard, however, users cannot change their minds because the Default Pushbutton is invoked on the downstroke of the Return key. Caution should be exercised when designing an application in which the user can make a mistake with a default action. Figure 4–12 shows a Default Pushbutton in its unselected and armed states.

A Default Pushbutton can be configured from the Pushbutton resource **XmNshowAsDefault.** This resource defaults to 1 and should not be changed. The visual result of this is a Pushbutton with a 1-pixel-thick outer ring surrounding it at a predetermined distance. An algorithm automatically assigns the distance between the Default Pushbutton's top and bottom shadows and its outer ring.

Default Pushbutton Unselected

Default Pushbutton Armed

FIGURE 4–12 A Default Pushbutton shown in its unselected and
armed states.

Like a Pushbutton, a Default Pushbutton will fill in its armed color. A Default Pushbutton should use the same margin settings as Pushbuttons. If
you keep the margins consistent, Default Pushbuttons will display themselves consistently with the other Pushbuttons. Figure 4–13 shows a Default Pushbutton's visual layout components.

Default Pushbuttons should always be located leftmost in the confirmation row at the bottom of any dialog box. Default Pushbuttons are usually
labeled "OK" in an OK/Cancel situation or "Apply" in an Apply/Close
situation. When used alone as simply "OK" or "Close," they should be
centered in the dialog box confirmation row. Figure 4–14 shows a Default Pushbutton aligned and positioned with other Pushbuttons in
a Dialog Box.

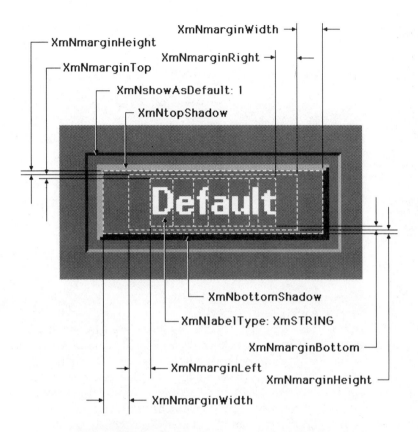

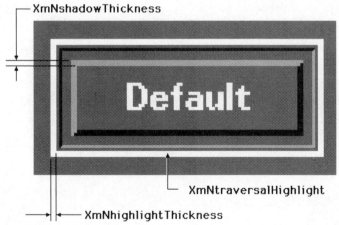

FIGURE 4–13 A Default Pushbutton's visual layout components.

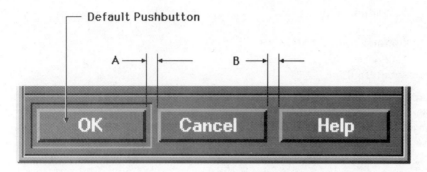

Dimension A should be equal to dimension B

FIGURE 4–14 A Default Pushbutton aligned and positioned with other Pushbuttons in a dialog box confirmation row.

Toggles

Toggles are primitive widgets that are often referred to as Checkboxes and Radiobuttons. These are typically used as state setters in which a set of choices must be made before invoking a task. The Toggle indicators can take the shape of either a diamond for Radiobuttons or a square for Checkboxes. Toggles are usually expected to be displayed with a Label attached to them; however, they can be displayed as just an indicator with no Labels or as Labels with no indicators. Because Toggle is the class name for both *"n* of many" and "1 of many" selections, I will refer to *"n* of many" as Checkboxes and "1 of many" as Radiobuttons. This will help to differentiate the two types of Toggles. Figure 4–15 shows the two types.

"n of many" selection

FIGURE 4–15 "One-of-many" toggles are referred to as Radiobuttons. "N-of-many" toggles are referred to as Checkboxes.

"1 of many" selection

Checkboxes —
"N of Many"

Toggles in Motif are used when single or multiple selections are required to set conditions for a task. Checkboxes are Toggle's "*n* of many" selection mode. When several changes must be made before a task can be carried out, Checkboxes would be the proper widgets to use. A Checkbox can also be used alone. Because the action of a Checkbox is to turn a setting on or off, it can be used alone and still make sense to the user. When selected, a Checkbox will respond by reversing the top and bottomshadows of its square indicator and will appear depressed. When selected, a Checkbox will fill the center of its indicator with its select color. Deselection can be made by selecting the same Checkbox indicator again. Selecting another Checkbox will not deselect a previous selection. It will simply add the new selection to the already selected Checkboxes. Checkboxes can at times be displayed as insensitive. Insensitive Checkboxes will be displayed with a 50-percent dithered Label. Figure 4–16 shows Checkboxes as unselected, selected, and insensitive.

Checkboxes are represented visually by square indicators. A Checkbox assigns its background color to the center of the square indicator. The background color is the same as that used as the background of the Checkbox's parent window. Its top shadow color is assigned to the left and top chamfers and its bottom shadow color is assigned to its bottom and right chamfers of the square indicator. The center of the Checkbox indicator changes to the select color when selected by the user.

Checkboxes are sized according to the font size used for their Labels. An algorithm determines the size of the Checkboxes so that they will look proportionally correct when used with Radiobuttons that use the same sized fonts. Checkboxes come by default with a 4-pixel space from the

Unselected

Selected

Insensitive

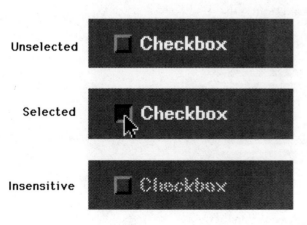

FIGURE 4–16 A Checkbox shown in its unselected, selected, and insensitive states.

right edge of the indicator's outer area to the left edge of the Label's left-most font cell. Depending on the font size that is used and the computer's display resolution, this dimension can be changed to achieve an appropriate distance in the resource **XmNspacing.** I would not change this, though, because 4 pixels is a visually acceptable distance for most font sizes. Figure 4–17 shows a Checkbox widget's visual layout components.

FIGURE 4–17 A Checkbox widget's visual layout components. Dimension A is equal to the height of the font cell. Dimension B (square indicator) is positioned as a result of an algorithm based on dimension A.

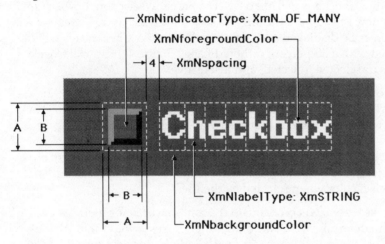

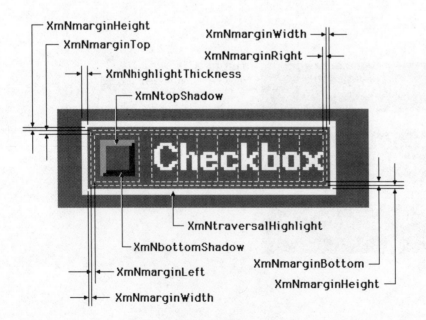

Radiobuttons—
"1 of Many"

Toggles are also called Radiobuttons when they are used to select one choice over another. Radiobuttons are Toggle's "1 of many" selection mode. Just like the buttons on a car radio from which it got its name, a Radiobutton allows a user to make only one selection at a time. Any new selection will deactivate the previously made selection. A single Radiobutton should not be represented in an interface. There must be a minimum of two Radiobuttons for the mental model of a Radiobutton (a one of many selection) to make any sense to the user. This functionality is enforced when Radiobuttons are used in the RowColumn manager RadioBox. When selected, a Radiobutton will reverse the top and bottom shadow colors in the indicator to show that it has responded, and it will fill in its center with its select color to show that the selection has been made. Deselection can be made by pressing on it again if the Radiobutton is set to allow "0 of many." Another selection has to be made to deselect the current Radiobutton selection. Figure 4–18 shows Radiobuttons as unselected, selected, and insensitive.

Radiobuttons are represented visually as diamond indicators. When a user selects a Radiobutton, the center of the indicator will fill with the select color. A Radiobutton assigns its background color to the center of the diamond indicator. The background color is the same as that used as the background of the Radiobutton's parent window. Its top shadow color is assigned to the top left and right chamfers and its bottom shadow color is assigned to the bottom left and right chamfers of the diamond indicator. The center of the Radiobutton indicator fills with the select color when selected by the user.

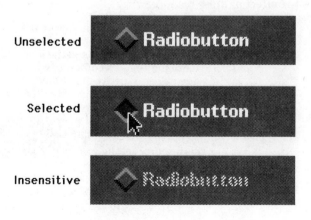

Unselected

Selected

Insensitive

FIGURE 4–18 A Radiobutton shown in its unselected, selected, and insensitive states.

The diamond indicator is sized from the font character cell height of the Radiobutton's Label. The width of the indicator is the same as its height. Radiobuttons come by default with a 4-pixel space from the right edge of the indicator to the left side of the Label. Depending on the font size that is used and the computer's display resolution, this dimension can be changed to achieve an appropriate distance in the resource **XmNspacing**. As in Checkboxes, I would not change this, because 4 pixels is a visually acceptable distance for most font sizes. Figure 4–19 shows Radiobutton widget layout components.

The size of a Toggle, whether a Checkbox or a Radiobutton, is determined by the size of the font character cells that are within its borders. Along with the size of the font used, the Toggle's margin height and margin width also determine the widget size. When a font of a new size replaces the current font, the margin height and margin width remain the same. This could cause the Toggle to appear misaligned with other widgets unless their fonts were changed also to match the Toggle's new font size. It is important to determine a margin height and width that would work well visually with a font size. Margin height and width can be changed if necessary.

When laying out a Toggle in line with other widgets, the height and the width, called margins, of the area surrounding the text must be adjusted so that the text can be lined up correctly with the text in other widgets. These margins are adjustable through resources that specify the distance from the text to the edge of the widget. These settings are specified in pixels.

A Toggle's margins are specified in the resources **XmNmarginHeight** (margin height) and **XmNmarginWidth** (margin width). These resources center Toggle's text and indicator from top to bottom and from side to side. These resources apply to both Radiobuttons and Checkboxes. The following list describes the effect of these resources:

XmNmarginHeight	This resource setting will specify the distance in pixels between the top edge of the top margin and the top edge of the Toggle's border. This pixel value will also specify the distance between the bottom edge of the bottom margin and the lower edge of the Toggle's border. Both of these distances will be set simultaneously.
XmNmarginWidth	This resource setting will specify the distance in pixels between the left edge of the left margin and the left edge of the Toggle's border. This pixel

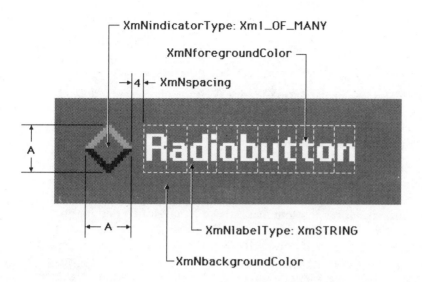

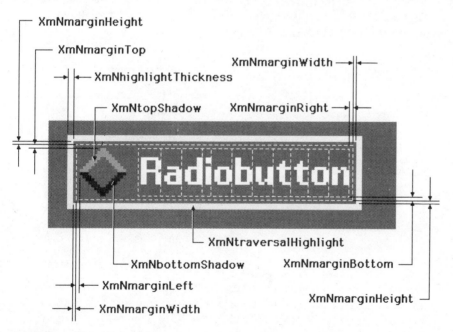

FIGURE 4–19 A Radiobutton widget's visual layout components. Dimension A is equal to the height of the font cell.

value will also specify the distance between the right edge of the right margin and the right edge of the Toggle's border. Both of these distances will be set simultaneously.

XmNmarginHeight and **XmNmarginWidth** are both set by default to 2 pixels and should remain unchanged for best visual results. These margins can be altered if more spacing is required between the Toggle's indicator and the Label with its outer widget edges.

Toggles can also be specified to position their Labels other than in the center. In this case, you will have to specify the other margins. These other margins are set using the resources **XmNmarginTop** (top margin), **XmNmarginBottom** (bottom margin), **XmNmarginLeft** (left margin), and **XmNmarginRight** (right margin). These will set each margin distance separately from the respective edge of the text and the corresponding edge of Toggle's margin height and width. These margin settings can be used in combination with or instead of using margin height and width. To use them instead of margin height and width, you must set **XmNmarginHeight** and **XmNmarginWidth** both to 0. The following list describes the effect of these resources:

XmNmarginTop
This resource setting will set the distance in pixels between the top side of the text font cells and the bottom edge of the upper margin height.

XmNmarginBottom
This resource setting will set the distance in pixels between the bottom side of the text font cells and the top edge of the lower margin height.

XmNmarginLeft
This resource setting will set the distance in pixels between the left side of the indicator and the right edge of the left margin width.

XmNmarginRight
This resource setting will set the distance in pixels between the right side of the text font cells and the left edge of the right margin width.

I would not recommend using these four margin resources too often unless your application requires some unusual alignment of Toggles to some other widget. If possible, stick to the simple method of specifying margin heights and widths. Figures 4–20 and 4–21 show the visual effect that the different margin resources have on Checkboxes and Radiobuttons.

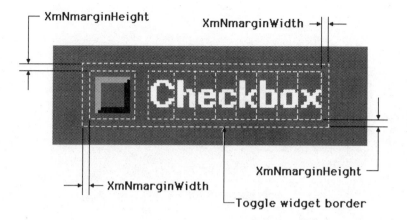

Toggle margin height & width only

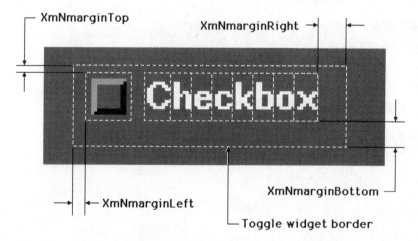

Toggle margin top, bottom, left, & right only

FIGURE 4–20 A Toggle's positioning is altered within its traversal highlight border when various margins are specified.

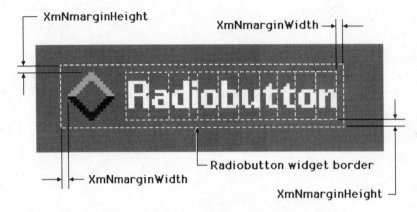

Radiobutton margin height and width only

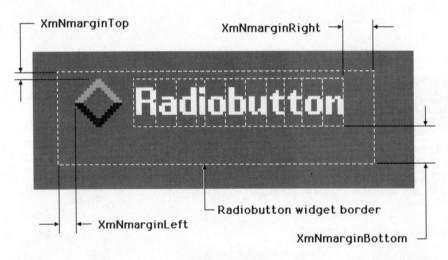

Radiobutton top, bottom, left, & right margins only

FIGURE 4–21 Radiobutton positioning is altered within its traversal highlight border when its various margins are specified.

Arrows

Arrows are primitive widgets that can be used as Pushbuttons to step through a list of choices or to step from one file to another. Arrows can also be used effectively to scroll through a list of items one at a time. For instance, names and addresses or lists of items that are viewed one at a time can be perused using Arrows. Figure 4–22 shows Arrows in their typical use.

Arrows are represented visually as arrows with a frame surrounding them. When selected, the Arrow image's top and bottom shadows reverse, giving the illusion that it has been depressed into the surface. Arrows assign their background color to the center of their triangular Arrow. An Arrow's top and bottom shadow colors change depending on the Arrow's orientation. Its surrounding rectangular frame colors are assigned as are those for a recessed widget. On this frame, the top shadow color is assigned to its bottom and right chamfer and the bottom shadow color is assigned to its left and top chamfer. The recessed background in which the Arrow sits is assigned the Arrow's select color.

Arrows can be sized to accommodate most situations. An Arrow's height is specified in the resource **XmNheight,** and its width is specified in **XmNwidth.** The values assigned to these resources include the shadow and traversal highlight thicknesses. The Arrow will be sized in proportion to the lower value if these two values are different. Minimally sized arrows tend to look the best in proportion and scale to the rest of the application window. I recommend that an Arrow value of 16 be assigned as both **XmNheight** and **XmNwidth.** Figure 4–23 shows the Arrow with its widget components.

Arrows can be displayed in four directions. The following list describes each Arrow direction that can be set in the XmArrow resource **XmNarrowDirection:**

XmARROW_UP	This sets the Arrow to point up.
XmARROW_DOWN	This sets the Arrow to point down.
XmARROW_LEFT	This sets the Arrow to point left.
XmARROW_RIGHT	This sets the Arrow to point right.

Figure 4–24 shows Arrow's four alternate directions.

FIGURE 4–22 Arrows as they are typically used.

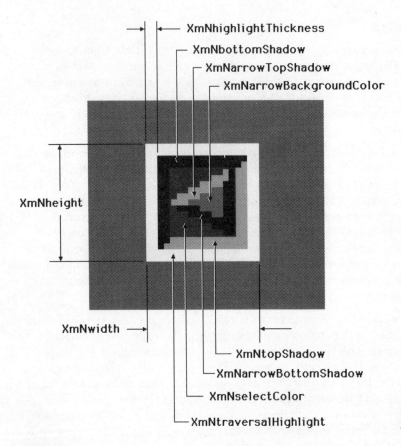

XmNhighlightThickness
XmNbottomShadow
XmNarrowTopShadow
XmNarrowBackgroundColor

XmNheight

XmNwidth

XmNtopShadow
XmNarrowBottomShadow
XmNselectColor
XmNtraversalHighlight

FIGURE 4–23 An Arrow widget's visual layout components.

 XmARROW_UP

 XmARROW_DOWN

 XmARROW_LEFT

 XmARROW_RIGHT

FIGURE 4–24 An Arrow's four alternate directions.

Cascade Buttons

Cascade Buttons are buttons that spawn MenuPanes. They are the link between two MenuPanes or the Menubar and a MenuPane. Cascade Buttons are the only widget that can have a Pulldown Menupane attached to it. They are used in Menubars as well as in Cascading MenuPanes.

Cascade Buttons are represented visually as two-dimensional Labels in Menubars and Menupanes and display their top and bottom frames as three-dimensional only when dragged upon for selection. When dragged upon, Cascade Buttons, like Pushbuttons, assign their background color as the flat area on the top. The top shadow color is assigned to the left and top chamfers, and the bottom shadow color is assigned to the bottom and right chamfers. These do not reverse when the Cascade Button is selected. Cascade Buttons can include a Label or a pixmap. Figure 4–25 shows a typical Cascade Button.

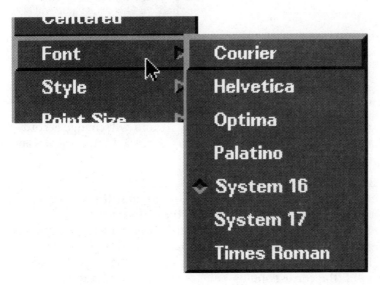

FIGURE 4–25 Cascade Buttons are typically used in Pulldown Menus for spawning cascading Menupanes.

A Cascade Button's margins are specified in the resources **XmNmarginHeight** (margin height) and **XmNmarginWidth** (margin width). These will center the Cascade Button's Label from top to bottom and from side to side. The following list describes the effect of these resources:

XmNmarginHeight	This resource setting will specify the distance in pixels between the top edge of the top margin and the inside edge of the Cascade Button's top shadow. This pixel value will also specify the distance between the bottom edge of the bottom margin and the inside edge of the Cascade Button's bottom shadow. Both of these distances will be set simultaneously.
XmNmarginWidth	This resource setting will specify the distance in pixels between the left edge of the left margin and the left inside edge of the Cascade Button's top shadow. This pixel value will also specify the distance between the right edge of the right margin and the right inside edge of the Cascade Button's bottom shadow. Both of these distances will be set simultaneously.

XmNmarginHeight defaults to 2 pixels and should remain unchanged. **XmNmarginWidth** defaults to a dynamic state and will change according to what is placed in it. Figure 4–26 shows a Cascade Button's visual layout components.

Cascade Buttons can also be specified to position their Labels other than in the center. In this case, you will have to specify the other margins. These other margins are specified through these resources: **XmNmarginTop** (top margin), **XmNmarginBottom** (bottom margin), **XmNmarginLeft** (left margin), and **XmNmarginRight** (right margin). These will set each margin distance separately from the respective edge of the text and the corresponding edge of the Cascade Button's margin height or margin width. These margin settings can be used in conjuction with or instead of margin height and width. It is up to the application developer to decide which will work best. To use these resources instead of margin height and width, you must set **XmNmarginHeight** and **XmNmarginWidth** both to 0. The following list describes each margin resource.

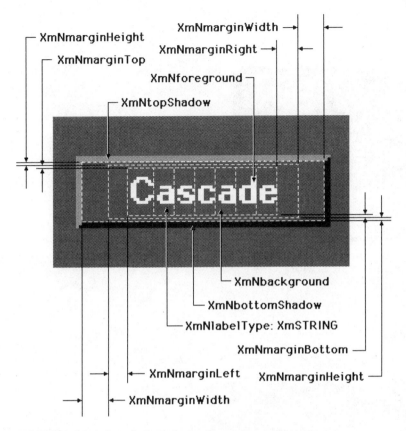

FIGURE 4–26 A Cascade Button's visual layout components.

XmNmarginTop	This resource setting will set the distance in pixels between the top side of the text font cells and the bottom edge of the upper margin height.
XmNmarginBottom	This resource setting will set the distance in pixels between the bottom side of the text font cells and the top edge of the lower margin height.
XmNmarginLeft	This resource setting will set the distance in pixels between the left side of the text font cells and the right edge of the left margin width.
XmNmarginRight	This resource setting will set the distance in pixels between the right side of the text font cells and the left edge of the right margin width.

Figure 4–27 shows a Cascade Button with its various margin adjustments.

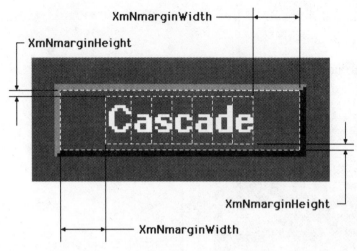

Cascade Button margin height & width only

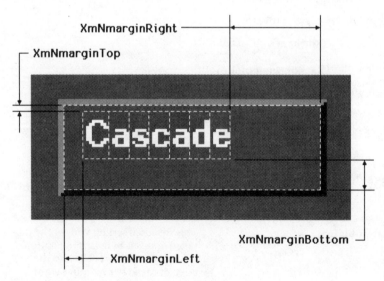

Cascade Button margin top, bottom, left, & right only

FIGURE 4–27 A Cascade Button's text positioning is altered when different margins are specified.

Cascade Buttons, when used in MenuPanes and Menubars, will hardly ever be required to align themselves horizontally with other widgets. Their margin resources **XmNmarginWidth** and **XmNmarginRight** default to a dynamic state so that the Menu Shell can do with Cascade Buttons what it pleases. **XmNmarginLeft** defaults to 0. This will allow the Label to remain left-justified regardless of how wide the MenuPane gets.

Cascade Buttons can be placed into three configurations. The type of menu configuration can be specified in the resource **XmNrowColumn Type.** The following are the three types:

XmMENU_PULLDOWN	This will make the RowColumn a Menupane.
XmMENU_POPUP	This will make the RowColumn a Popup Menu.
XmMENU_BAR	This will make the RowColumn a Menubar.

Separators

Separators are widgets that display themselves as visual separations between areas in the application. They can be used anywhere in an application. They are most handy as visual separations of functional areas as well as separations of topical choices, such as in a Menupane. Separators are most commonly used in Pulldown Menus between topic areas, but they can also be used in application windows and dialog boxes. Figure 4–28 shows a typical use for a Separator.

Separators can be represented visually in several different ways. The type of separator can be specified in the resource **XmNseparatorType.** The following two Separator styles are preferred for use as separations of functional areas:

XmSHADOW_ETCHED_IN	This setting displays a double-etched line, giving the visual effect of a line etched into the surface of the background. When a Separator is displayed in a horizontal position, the top line is the bottom shadow color and the bottom line is the top shadow color. When it is displayed in a vertical position, the left line is the bottom shadow and the right line is the top shadow color.

Separators used to divide functional areas.

Separators also used to group selections in Menupanes.

FIGURE 4–28 A Separator shown spanning a work area.

XmSHADOW_ETCHED_OUT   This setting displays a double-etched line, giving the visual effect of a line etched out from the surface of the background. When a Separator is displayed in a horizontal position, the top line is the top shadow color and the bottom line is the bottom shadow color. When it is displayed in a vertical position, the left line is the top shadow and the right line is the bottom shadow color.

I recommend the use of the Separator set at **XmSHADOW_ETCHED_IN** as the Separator of choice for separating functional areas. The "Shadow Etched In" appearance provides a subtle and aesthetically pleasing scribed line. This type of Separator should be used in applications as well as in all Pulldown Menu separations. Figure 4–29 shows a Separator with its components.

FIGURE 4–29 A Separator's etched styles.

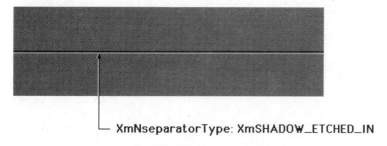

XmNseparatorType: XmSHADOW_ETCHED_IN

XmNseparatorType: XmSHADOW_ETCHED_OUT

XmNorientation: XmHORIZONTAL

The thickness of the etched line is specified in the resource
XmNshadowThickness. For best visual results, I recommend a setting of
2 pixels, which will result in a Separator with a 1-pixel top shadow and
a 1-pixel bottom shadow. The space between the ends of a Separator widget and its drawn line should default to 0 in the resource **XmNmargin.**
A Separator should extend to the ends of its area without any space between the drawn line and the end of the Separator widget. If this is not
the case, be sure that this resource is set to 0. In horizontal position,
this space is between the left and right ends of the line drawn and the
edges of the Separator. In vertical position, this space is between the ends
of the drawn line and the top and bottom edges of the Separator.
Figure 4–30 shows where the margin occurs in a Separator, as well as the
thickness of a Separator.

Separators can be displayed either horizontally or vertically. In either orientation, the top and bottom shadows will be repositioned automatically so that the Separator consistently looks as though it is being lit from
the top and left. This is the case whether the Separators are displayed
etched in or etched out. The orientation of Separators can be specified
in the resource **XmNorientation.** This can be set to **XmVERTICAL**
for a vertical orientation or to **XmHORIZONTAL** for a horizontal orientation. Figure 4–31 shows the two Separator orientations.

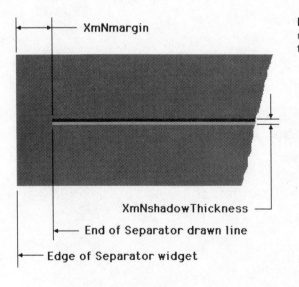

XmNmargin

XmNshadowThickness

End of Separator drawn line

Edge of Separator widget

FIGURE 4–30 A Separator's
margin and thickness specifications.

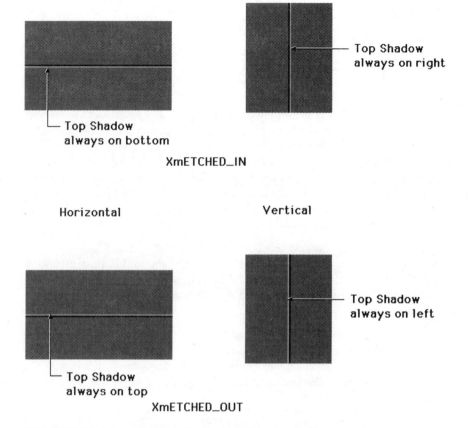

FIGURE 4–31 A Separator orientated horizontally and vertically.

The following Separator types, although provided in Motif, should not be used to separate functional areas. They should be used in image or graphical areas that require separation. These types are colored with the foreground color and do not represent a three-dimensional effect that physically separates major areas.

XmSINGLE_LINE	This setting displays a single line.
XmDOUBLE_LINE	This setting displays a double line.
XmSINGLE_DASHED_LINE	This setting displays a single dashed line.
XmDOUBLE_DASHED_LINE	This setting displays a double dashed line.
XmNO_LINE	This setting displays no line.

Frames

A Frame is a manager widget that has a set of top and bottom shadows and can contain only one child widget. This child widget can be either a primitive widget such as a Pushbutton or a container widget such as a RowColumn manager. If the Frame's child is a container widget, the container widget can have within it as many children as it can handle. If a primitive widget such as a Pushbutton is placed as a Frame's child, it will be the only widget that can be placed in the Frame. A Frame can be used to give the illusion that the widget is surrounded with a beveled edge, thus giving it the three-dimensional look of a raised or a recessed area or a look of an area defined by an etched line. These borders come in four styles, which are "Frame In," "Frame Out," "Etched In," and "Etched Out." A Frame can be used also for creating a raised or lowered slab to give a three-dimensional appearance to pixmap images.

In and Out Frames

In and Out frames are best used to surround a Paned Window or any other grouping of widgets. The thickness of the top and bottom shadows is set by the application developer. This widget can be used to make its child widget appear tobe on a raised area (Frame Out) or in a recessed area (Frame In).

The Frame widget is represented visually as a rectangle with its left and top chamfers being the top shadow and its right and bottom chamfers being the bottom shadow. The area within the Frame's top and bottom shadows is assigned the background color. Figure 4–32 shows In and Out Frames.

In and Out Frames can be displayed in two styles. The style choice can be set in the resource **XmNshadowType** in the XmFrame Resource Set. The following list describes each style:

XmSHADOW_IN   This creates the "Frame In" look, which gives the illusion that the panel within the Frame is recessed into its parent background.

XmSHADOW_OUT   This creates the "Frame Out" look, which gives the illusion that the panel within the Frame is raised from its parent background.

The colors for a Frame are the most convincing when you use the same color set as that used for the Frame's parent. A Frame can also be used to surround a Paned Window to give it the look of a slab within the application window frame that surrounds it. For this purpose, "Shadow Out" would give the best visual result. Figure 4–33 shows Frame Out with its widget components.

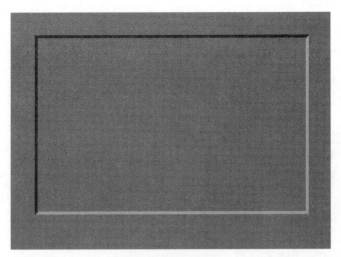

Frame "Shadow In"
XmSHADOW_IN

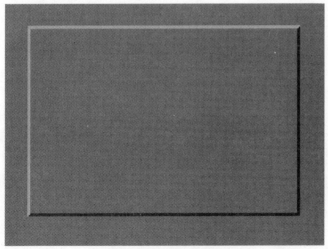

Frame "Shadow Out"
XmSHADOW_OUT

FIGURE 4–32 A Frame shown as "Shadow In" and "Shadow Out."

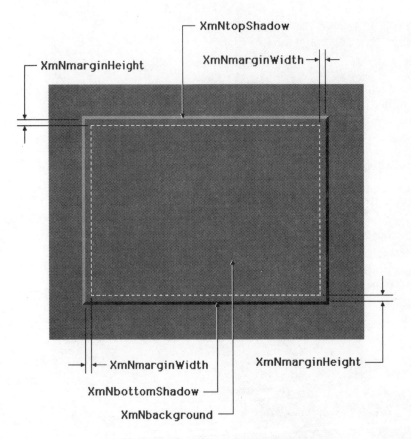

XmNshadowType: XmSHADOW_OUT

FIGURE 4–33 A Frame "Shadow Out" with its visual layout components.

Shadow thicknesses of 2 pixels generally look best on In and Out Frames. You be the judge on what to choose; however, the shadow thicknesses should be consistent throughout your application. Figure 4–34 shows how much Frames can differ in appearance depending on what thickness you choose.

XmNshadowThickness. 1

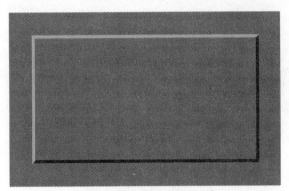

XmNshadowThickness: 2

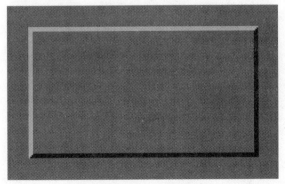

XmNshadowThickness: 3

FIGURE 4–34 Various thicknesses can alter the appearance of a Frame. This example shows a Frame "Shadow Out."

Etched Frames

Etched frames are best used to contain any type or set of widgets to give them a sense of grouping. Such widgets should be used only to group a set of visually similar or dissimilar widgets related by context. For instance, a set of Text widgets can be grouped together in a RowColumn manager and placed in an Etched Frame. The Etched Frame gives the illusion of being scribed into the background panel if you select "Etched In" or as being popped out as a fence by selecting "Etched Out." Figure 4–35 shows an Etched In Frame and an Etched Out Frame.

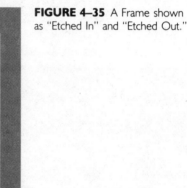

FIGURE 4–35 A Frame shown as "Etched In" and "Etched Out."

Frame "Etched In"
XmSHADOW_ETCHED_IN

Frame "Etched Out"
XmSHADOW_ETCHED_OUT

Etched Frames can be displayed in two styles. The style choice can be set in the resource **XmNshadowType** in the XmFrame Resource Set. The following list describes each style:

XmSHADOW_ETCHED_IN   This creates the "Etched In" look, which gives the illusion that the Frame surrounding the panel within the Frame is scribed into its parent background.

XmSHADOW_ETCHED_OUT   This creates the "Etched Out" look. This gives the illusion that the Frame surrounding the panel within the Frame is popped out like a fine-lined fence on its parent background.

The shadow colors for frame are the most convincing when set to the top and bottom shadow and background colors of its parent . Figure 4–36 shows Frame "Etched In" with its widget components.

FIGURE 4–36 A Frame "Etched In" with its visual layout components.

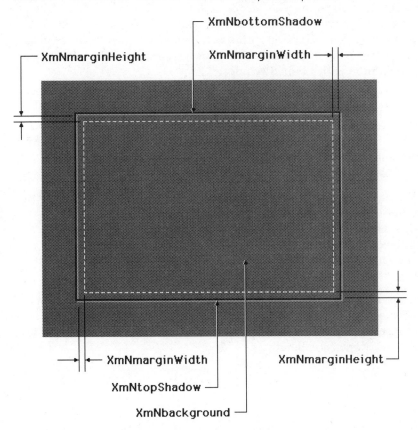

XmNshadowType: XmSHADOW_ETCHED_IN

A shadow thickness of 1 pixel looks best on Etched In and Etched Out Frames. Any thickness above 1 pixel will not look convincing as an etched line. However, if you choose to set this to a thicker pixel setting, use it consistently in your application. Figure 4–37 shows how much your Etched frames can differ in appearance depending on what thickness you choose.

Paned Windows

A Paned Window is a composite window that stretches and shrinks in height via direct manipulation by the user. A Paned Window lays out its children vertically and sizes itself according to its widest child. The other children are forced to the resultant size of the Paned Window.

A Paned Window is represented visually as two adjustable areas (panes) with an "etched-in" line separating the two panes. At the separation between it and another pane is a sash whose size can be specified by the application designer. This sash resembles a small Pushbutton and is located between the two panes. The user can adjust the size of each pane by selecting the sash with the mouse and moving the sash up or down. As the sash is moved, one pane will shrink as the other one grows. The application window will not change in size while this is done. Figure 4–38 shows an application with a Paned Window.

A minimum and a maximum size should be specified for each pane. This prevents the user from resizing the pane below its minimum size or beyond its maximum size. A minimum size could be the height of a row of Pushbuttons. A maximum size could be the height of a Scrolled Window. These dimensions can be specified in the resource **XmNmaximum** and **XmNminimum.**

A Paned Window lays out its children within its margins. The margins provide a visual area that can be specified in the resources **XmNmarginHeight** and **XmNmarginWidth. XmNmarginHeight** specifies an equal dimension between Paned Window's children and its top and bottom edges. **XmNmarginWidth** specifies an equal dimension between its children and its left and right edges.

The distance between Paned Windows can be specified in the resource **XmNspacing.** This defaults to 8 pixels, which allows the sash and the separator between panes to remain displayed. Figure 4–39 shows a Paned Window's dimension details.

XmNshadowThickness: 1

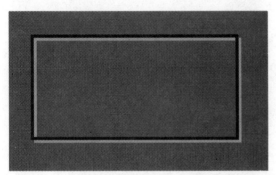

XmNshadowThickness: 2

XmNshadowThickness: 3

FIGURE 4–37 Various thicknesses can alter the appearance of a Frame. This example shows a Frame "Etched In."

FIGURE 4–38 Paned Windows are used to separate an application window's work area.

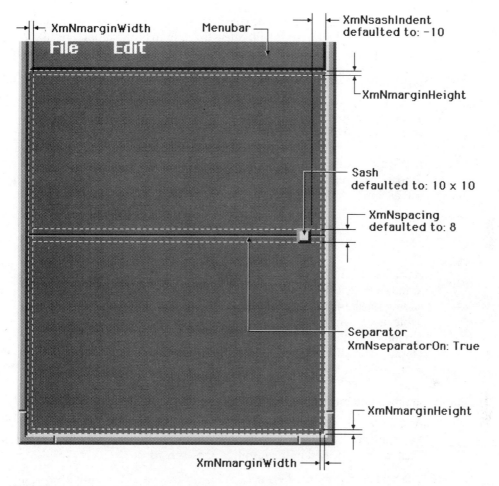

FIGURE 4–39 A Paned Window's visual layout components.

The height and width of a Paned Window's sash, as well as its location along the bottom of each pane, can be specified. Its height can be specified in the resource **XmNsashHeight.** This defaults to 10 pixels. I recommend that this dimension be changed to 6. The sash width can be specified in the resource **XmNsashWidth.** This also defaults to 10 pixels. For best aesthetic quality, I recommend that this dimension be equal to the width of the Scrollbars used in your application. If you happen not to have any ScrollBars in your application, specify 12 pixels for this dimension. Now that the dimension of the sash is set to a visually pleasing proportion, its location will complete the visual quality of the Paned Window.

The location of the sash can be specified in the resource **XmNsashIndent.** A positive pixel dimension will cause the sash to be positioned from the left side of the Paned Window. A negative pixel dimension will cause the sash to be positioned from the right side of the Paned Window. This dimension defaults to -10, which positions the sash 10 pixels from the right edge of the pane. I recommend that this dimension be changed to be equal to the dimension by which your vertical Scrollbars are offset from the right edge of the Paned Window. If your application has no Scrollbars, set this resource to -4. This will allow the sash to be positioned close to the right edge of the pane, as well as leaving enough room around it for easy selection. Figure 4–40 shows a Paned Window's optimum sash dimensions.

Scales

A Scale is used to indicate a value from within a range of values — for example, a Scale could be used to adjust a volume control. It is basically a sliding mechanism that is moved by the user until the proper setting is achieved. It can be set to display graduating numeric information simultaneously while being adjusted. A Scale can also be used as an indicator of graduating information. So although it can be used for setting volume, it can also display the current volume level as well. The Scale incorporates a dynamically changing Label that shows its reading as the slider is grabbed and moved. Figure 4–41 shows a Scale widget and its typical use.

A Scale can also be used as a display-only indicator, like a thermometer. You can specify whether the user can interactively modify a Scale's value. This can be specified in the resource **XmNsensitive.**

The Scale is represented visually as a constant size slider bar within a recessed channel. Its length and its graduation is determined by the software developer. Its colors are assigned in the following manner. The foreground color is assigned to the Scale's dynamically changing Label.The background color is assigned to the top of the slider. The Scale's top shadow is the lower and right chamfer, and its bottom shadow is the upper and left chamfer. The trough area defaults to the select color, which is derived automatically based on the background color.

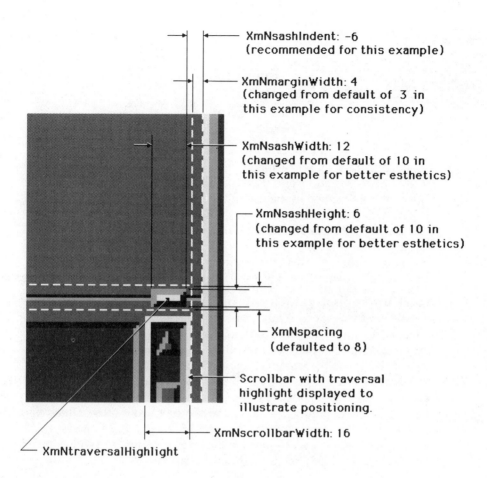

XmNsashIndent: –6
(recommended for this example)

XmNmarginWidth: 4
(changed from default of 3 in
this example for consistency)

XmNsashWidth: 12
(changed from default of 10 in
this example for better esthetics)

XmNsashHeight: 6
(changed from default of 10 in
this example for better esthetics)

XmNspacing
(defaulted to 8)

Scrollbar with traversal
highlight displayed to
illustrate positioning.

XmNscrollbarWidth: 16

XmNtraversalHighlight

When aligning Sash with vertical Scrollbar:

XmNsashWidth= XmNscrollbarWidth minus 4
if Scrollbar traversal highlight thickness = 2.

FIGURE 4-40 A Paned Window's optimum sash dimensions.

FIGURE 4–41 A Scale widget is used for direct control of adjusting as well as for display functions.

The height of a Scale is specified in the resource **XmNscaleHeight.** This height includes shadow and traversal highlight thicknesses. A Scale's width can be specified in the resource **XmNscaleWidth.** This width includes shadow and traversal highlight thicknesses. In specifying these values, remember that **XmNscaleHeight** will always specify the height (top to bottom length), regardless of the Scale's orientation. The resource **XmNscaleWidth** will always specify the width (side to side), regardless of the Scale's orientation. Figure 4–42 shows a Scale's layout components.

A Scale can be displayed vertically or horizontally. Its orientation can be specified in the resource **XmNorientation.** When specifying a Scale's orientation, remember to reassign the values in **XmNscaleHeight** and **XmNscaleWidth,** or the visual result will assign the opposite values for each resource. For example, if your Scale is horizontal and **XmNscaleWidth** is set to 100 and **XmNscaleHeight** is set to 10, the result will be a Scale that is 100 pixels from side to side and 10 pixels high. If the Scale's orientation were changed to be vertical and these values were not changed, the result would be a vertical Scale that is 100 pixels wide and 10 pixels tall. This will force your Scale to look short and wide. The following should be specified for either orientation:

XmVERTICAL	This setting orients a Scale vertically.
XmHORIZONTAL	This setting orients a Scale horizontally.

Figure 4–43 shows a Scale in both orientations.

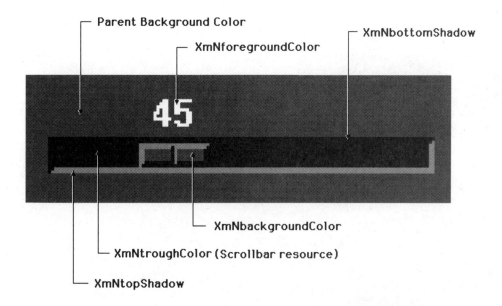

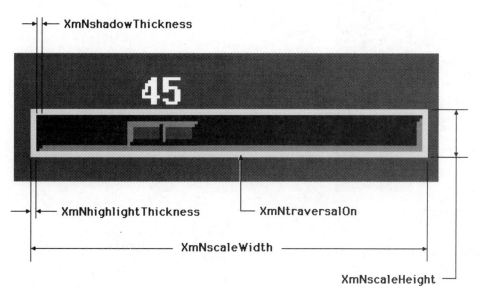

FIGURE 4–42 A Scale's visual layout components.

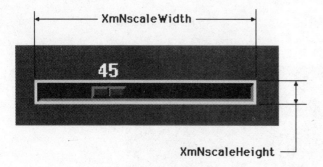

XmNorientation: XmHORIZONTAL

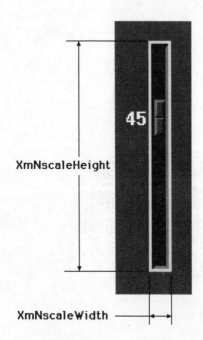

XmNorientation: XmVERTICAL

FIGURE 4–43 A Scale shown in both horizontal and vertical orientations.

Drawn Buttons

A Drawn Button is an empty widget window surrounded by a shadow border. It can have Pushbutton input semantics while providing a graphics area within its shadow border. The Drawn Button can have in its graphic area anything other than text or pixmaps. It is a window that can have images or animation in it.

A Drawn Button looks similar to a Pushbutton. Unlike Pushbuttons, though, Drawn Buttons can be displayed with a variety of border styles. As in a Pushbutton, a Drawn Button's margin height and width determine the distance between the graphic area and the inside edges of the Drawn Button's borders.

Drawn Buttons, like Pushbuttons, assign their background color as the flat area on the top. The top shadow color is assigned to the left and top chamfers, and the bottom shadow color is assigned to the bottom and right chamfers when the Drawn Button is displayed in its unselected state. These colors are reversed when the Drawn Button is selected. Figure 4–44 shows a typical Drawn Button.

FIGURE 4–44 A Drawn Button.

The margin height can be specified in pixels in the resource **XmNmarginHeight.** This will assign the specified pixel dimension at both the top and the bottom of the graphic image. The margin width can be specified in pixels in the resource **XmNmarginWidth.** This will assign the specified pixel dimension at both the right and the left of the graphic image. The following list describes which margins will be set in a Drawn Button:

XmNmarginHeight   This resource setting will specify the distance in pixels between the top edge of the top margin and the inside edge of a Drawn Button's top shadow. This pixel dimension will also specify the distance between the bottom edge of the bottom margin and the inside edge of a Drawn Button's bottom shadow. Both of these distances will be set simultaneously.

XmNmarginWidth	This resource setting will specify the distance in pixels between the left edge of the left margin and the left inside edge of a Drawn Button's top shadow. This pixel value will also specify the distance between the right edge of the right margin and the right inside edge of a Drawn Button's bottom shadow. Both of these distances will be set simultaneously.

Figure 4–45 shows the dimension details of a Drawn Button.

Drawn Buttons can also be specified so that their images are positioned somewhere other than in the center. In this case, you will have to specify the other margins, using the following resources: **XmNmarginTop** (top margin), **XmNmarginBottom** (bottom margin), **XmNmarginLeft** (left margin), and **XmNmarginRight** (right margin). These will set each margin distance based on the appropriate edge of the text and the corresponding margin height and widths. These margin settings can be used instead of or in conjunction with margin height and width. It is up to the application designer to decide which will work best. To use them instead of margin height and width, you must set **XmNmarginHeight** and **XmNmarginWidth** both to 0. The following list describes these margin settings:

XmNmarginTop	This resource setting will specify the distance in pixels between the top edge of the graphic area and the bottom edge of the upper margin height.
XmNmarginBottom	This resource setting will specify the distance in pixels between the bottom edge of the graphic area and the top edge of the lower margin height.
XmNmarginLeft	This resource setting will specify the distance in pixels between the left edge of the graphic area and the right edge of the left margin width.
XmNmarginRight	This resource setting will specify the distance in pixels between the right edge of the graphic area and the left edge of the right margin width.

Figure 4–46 shows the varying image positioning you can achieve by specifying different margins.

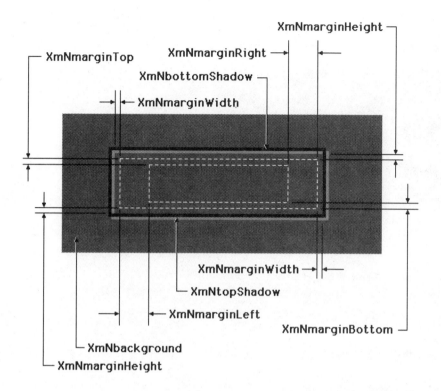

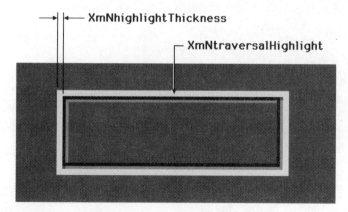

FIGURE 4–45 A Drawn Button's visual layout components.

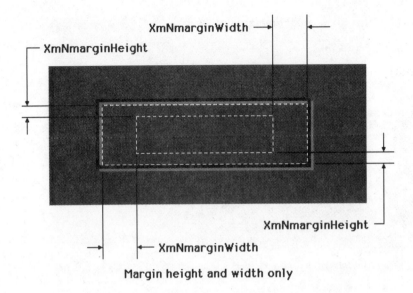

Margin height and width only

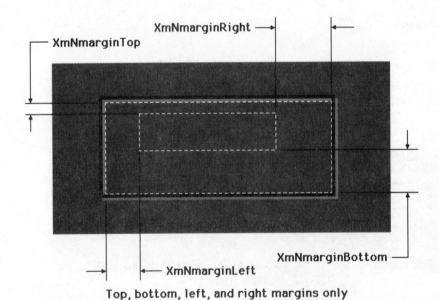

Top, bottom, left, and right margins only

FIGURE 4–46 A Drawn Button's image positioning is altered by specifying varying margins.

The Drawn Button's various styles of borders can be specified in the resource **XmNshadowType.** The border style can be selected from the following.

XmSHADOW_IN	This setting draws the top and bottom shadows as if they were inset into the background. This is done by drawing the shadows reversed.
XmSHADOW_OUT	This setting draws the top and bottom shadows as if they were protruding from the surface of the background. This is done by drawing the shadows in the same manner as in a Pushbutton.
XmSHADOW_ETCHED_IN	This setting draws the borders as a double line etched into the background. This gives the effect of a flush-edged Pushbutton etched into the surface of the background. The total thickness of the double line is determined by the specification assigned to **XmNshadowThickness.**
XmSHADOW_ETCHED_OUT	This setting draws the borders as a double line etched out from the background. This gives the effect of a scribed line popping out from the surface of the background. The total thickness of the double line is determined by the specification assigned to **XmNshadowThickness.**

The shadow thickness will affect the visual quality of the various borders. If you are using SHADOW_IN or SHADOW_OUT, I recommend setting the border to 2 pixels, as is the default for Pushbuttons. If using SHADOW_ETCHED_IN or SHADOW_ETCHED_OUT, set the border to 2 pixels. This will assign 1 pixel to both the top and the bottom shadows and will provide a refined etched look. Figure 4–47 shows the various border styles of a Drawn Button.

Menubars

Menubars serve an important function in application windows. They display the topics of most or all of the functions that are available in an application. When selected, the items in a Menubar spawn Pulldown Menus that display functions or states that can be applied to the current work in an application. The disclosure of each of these functions by selecting each Menubar item serves to acquaint the novice user to the capabilities of an application. To the experienced user, Menubars are helpful as

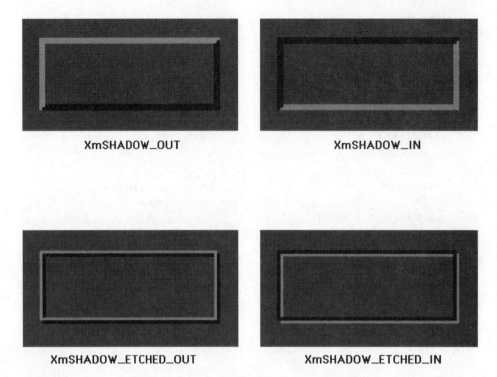

FIGURE 4–47 A Drawn Button can be configured with various border styles.

organizers that keep functions hidden until needed. Menubar selections should be displayed consistently with other applications. This allows the user to recognize similar functions while learning new functions unique to the application.

A Menubar is a manager widget that employs a RowColumn manager to set its children Cascade Button widgets in a horizontal row. Menubars can be created by using the convenience resource **XmCreateMenuBar.** They are configured to display topical information of major function categories in a row. The children widgets that are contained in the Menubar are Cascade Button widgets that link the Menubar to Pulldown Menus. Each topic in the Menubar looks like a Label until it is selected with the mouse pointer. When selected, the Cascade Button will appear to pop out, showing its Frame in the Frame Out position, and a Pulldown Menu will be spawned under it. Figure 4–48 shows a typical Menubar.

The horizontal spacing of the children in the Menubar is specified in the RowColumn resource **XmNspacing.** This value defaults to 0 and should not be changed. The child widgets are spaced right next to one another. This setting is fine, because the top and bottom shadows of each selection will appear only one at a time. The Menubar's Cascade Buttons are also placed as close to one another as possible for space efficiency. Figure 4–49 shows the recommended spacing for a Menubar's children.

Each Cascade Button in the Menubar should follow the same design guidelines as Pushbuttons. The margin height and width of these child widgets should be consistent with those of Pushbuttons used in the same application. Each Cascade Button child should also have the same dimension for its margin widths, regardless of the variation in the length of its Label. This consistent margin dimension will be added to either side of each Cascade Button's Label and will give your Menubar a uniform and refined look. A Label's margin width, set in **XmNmarginWidth,** defaults to 2 pixels. This should be increased when Labels are used in Cascade Buttons in a Menubar. A margin width of 2 just isn't enough of a horizontal distance to separate each Menu topic visually when the Cascade Button is displayed in its unselected position. A margin width of 8 pixels should be specified instead for each Cascade Button's margin width. This will distance each Menubar choice, avoiding the confusion resulting when Menubar choices appear like multiple words. As a result, the children widgets will retain their own unique overall width dimension and will provide a consistent distance between each Cascade Button's Label. I do not recommend achieving this distance between Menubar Labels by increasing the value in the **XmNspacing** resource. Although this will space the Labels farther in the unselected state, selecting a Cascade Button will show its Frames too close to its text. Figure 4–50 shows the difference between spacing Menubar choices when spawned.

Menubars are represented visually as a row of text selections that, when clicked upon with the mouse, force their Frames to appear in the Frame Out position without darkening the area surrounding text with the user/

FIGURE 4–48 A typical Menubar.

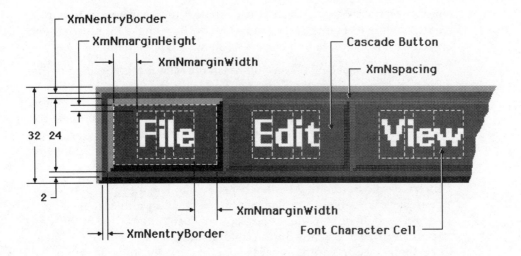

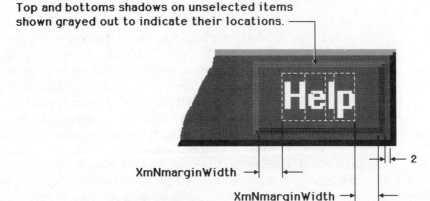

FIGURE 4–49 The recommended spacing for a Menubar's children. This view shows all ripples on to show spacing. In reality, ripples will appear one selection at a time.

select color. This popping out of the Menu selection indicates that the selection has been made and that a Pulldown Menu will appear from it. As the user moves the mouse cursor down the Pulldown Menu while pressing the mouse button, the menu selections in the Pulldown Menu will ripple out at each selection. This revealing of the Frame gives the feeling of the selections "rippling" as the user traverses the selections using the mouse.

This sensation of rippling through Menu selections is very useful for indicating which choices currently can be selected. This progressive disclosure of choices allows the user to better understand the capabilities of an

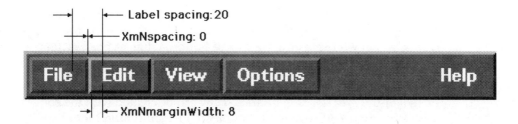

Recommended method of spacing Cascade Button
Labels through specifying XmNmarginWidth.

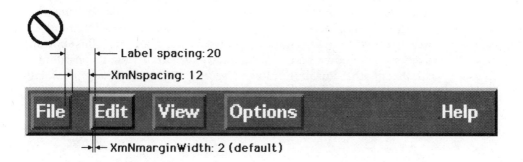

Not recommended to space Cascade Button Labels by increasing
resource XmNspacing.

FIGURE 4–50 Shows the difference between spacing Menubar choices by specifying the
XmNspacing resource and by using margin width resources.

application. Without having to try out every function, the user has had
a chance to view the choices available. If a situation should come up while
using the application, the user, having had prior exposure to its capabilities, might remember the needed option.

Pulldown Menus

Pulldown Menus, also referred to as Menupanes, are manager widgets
that use a RowColumn widget to contain button children. Pulldown
Menus are activated from a Menubar and display choices related to the
Menubar topic. As in the Menubar, the Menupane selections "ripple"

(show their Frames) when the user drags each Pulldown Menu choice. The rippling effect highlights one selection at a time when the user drags on a selection while pressing the mouse button. When a choice is decided upon, the user must release the mouse button to invoke that choice.

Pulldown Menus can have as children Pushbuttons, Toggle Buttons, Drawn Buttons, or Cascade Buttons. They can be created with the convenience function **XmCreateMenuPulldown.** Pushbuttons in MenuPane are displayed differently from regular Pushbuttons in other parts of an application. Just as in Menubars, the Pushbuttons are displayed as Labels until they are selected using the mouse. When selected, the Pushbutton's top and bottom shadows will appear in the Frame Out position until released. Unlike regular Pushbuttons, Pushbuttons in Pulldown Menus should have Labels that are left- justified. Selections that invoke an action should display plain Labels. Selections that spawn a dialog box should display a Label with ellipses (three sequential dots) after the text. These ellipses are considered to be the standard symbol that indicates that this Menu selection will spawn a dialog box. Each Pushbutton selection in Pulldown Menus should have its margin height consistent with that of other Pushbuttons and Cascade Buttons in the Menubar. Figure 4–51 shows how a Pulldown Menu is spawned from the Menubar.

FIGURE 4–51 A Pulldown Menu spawned from a Menubar.

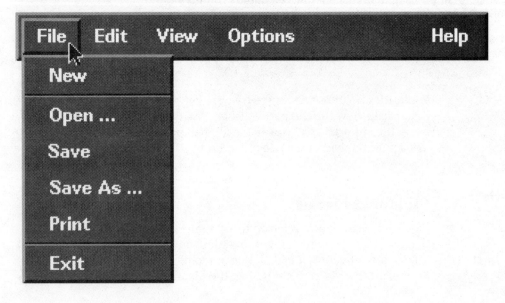

A Cascade Button is the other type of child in Pulldown Menus. Cascade Buttons are used for selections that will spawn other Menupanes. When Cascade Buttons are used in Pulldown Menus, a submenu will be attached to them. The **XmNmarginBottom, XmNmarginRight,** and **XmNmarginTop** resources will enlarge to accept a cascading arrow pixmap called **XmNcascadePixmap.**

The vertical spacing of the children in the Menubar is specified in the RowColumn resource **XmNspacing.** This value defaults to 1 pixel in a vertical orientation. I recommend that this setting be changed to 0 pixels. This would space the child widgets right above and below one another and make more efficient use of the vertical Menupane space. This setting will work fine, because the top and bottom shadows of each selection will only appear one at a time. If necessary, you can change this setting to another specification. Figure 4–52 shows a Pulldown Menu's various components.

FIGURE 4–52 A Menupane's various components include Pushbuttons that display their shadows when dragged to and Separators that separate functional groupings.

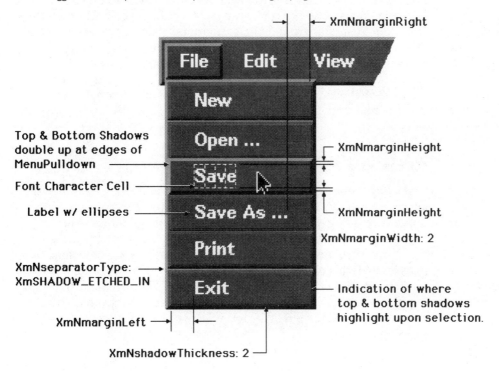

The Pulldown Menu is represented visually as a flat pane with a Frame-Out-style top and bottom shadow surrounding it. It assigns the top shadow color to its left and top chamfers and the bottom shadow color to its bottom and right chamfers. The rippling effect is caused by the individual Pushbuttons revealing their frames in the Frame Out mode when they are dragged upon with the mouse. Pulldown Menu selections can be grouped visually by topic or function by inserting Separators between the groups. Grouping within Separators is especially recommended when the group of Menu choices incorporates Toggles or Cascade Buttons. This creates a clear visual separation of the groups and helps the user to scan the Pulldown Menu choices quickly. The Separator that I suggest as the most visually successful is the "Etched In" separator. The Separator should run across the Pulldown Menu fully from side to side. This Separator should be specified to 2 pixels for the best visual quality.

Pulldown Menus automatically manage themselves in displaying information within each Pushbutton selection. The first column displays Toggles for sections of the Pulldown Menus that are used for state setters. A choice of a Radiobutton diamond indicator for "1 of many" selections or a Checkbox square indicator for "n of many" selections is displayed in this area. The second or middle column is reserved for text or a bitmapped image. If a bitmapped image is desired, it must be limited to a two-color image. The two colors can be two different colors from the Pulldown Menu foreground and background colors if preferred. Text in this area is restricted to the foreground color on the background color. The third column is reserved for displaying the arrow pixmap that indicates that a Cascading Menupane will be spawned from this selection. Figure 4–53 shows a Menupane's three columns, as determined by its RowColumn manager.

Cascading Menus

Cascading Menus are used for menu selections that require additional alternatives from which to choose in order to invoke a command or to set a state. Cascading Menus should be used to further define a selection that is being made from the Pulldown Menu. It should not be designed in such a way that a user must make several passes through the same steps in order to decide on a selection. Cascading Menus are best utilized to set states instead of to invoke functions. From Pulldown Menus, Cascading Menus are displayed by dragging upon a selection that has an arrow displayed at the right of the text selection. Figure 4–54 shows a typical Cascading Menu.

Cascade indicator column →   ←

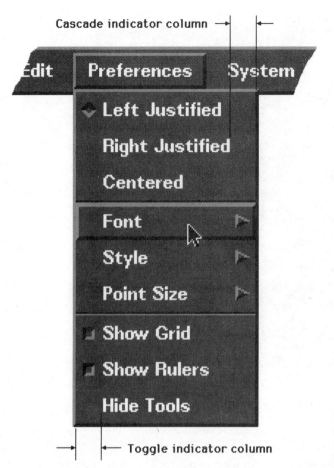

Toggle indicator column

FIGURE 4–53 A Menupane is divided automatically into three columns by its RowColumn manager.

Cascading Menus are represented visually as identical to Pulldown Menus. The only functional difference is that they are spawned from other Pulldown Menus or Cascading Menus when a Cascade Button is selected. This type of Cascading Menu is spawned next to the selection on the previous Pulldown Menus. After a slight delay, a new Menupane is spawned that contains more Menu choices. The selections in Cascading Menus should be comprised of choices that further enhance the selection of the previous Menu selection. They should not be selections that are unrelated to the Menu choice that spawned the Cascading Menu. Figure 4–55 shows a selection made from a Cascading Menu.

Cascading Menus could spawn other Cascading Menus. The application designer should set limits on how far a Cascading Menu will continue. Motif does not enforce any technical limits as to how many Cascading

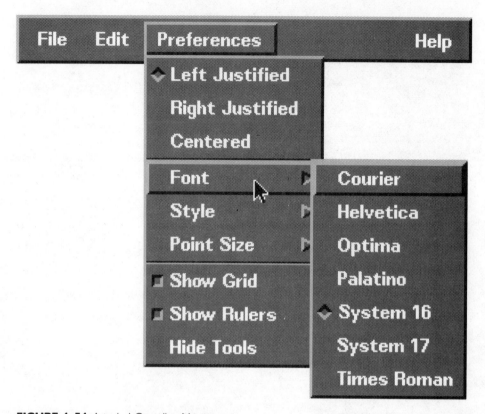

FIGURE 4–54 A typical Cascading Menu.

Menus can be spawned. I would recommend that a Pulldown Menu not cascade more than twice from its origin. This amounts to a total of three consecutive Menupanes at any one time. More than three consecutive cascading Menupanes are difficult for the user to comprehend. Long Cascading Menus can also cause strain on the hand that is pressing the mouse button.

Option Menus

An Option Menu allows an alternate way of making a "1 of many" selection other than using Radiobuttons or a List. This is especially desirable when the selection to be made is from a rather long list of choices. Unlike Radiobuttons or Lists, Option Menus make more efficient use of space when in their unselected state. Option Menus should be used when the

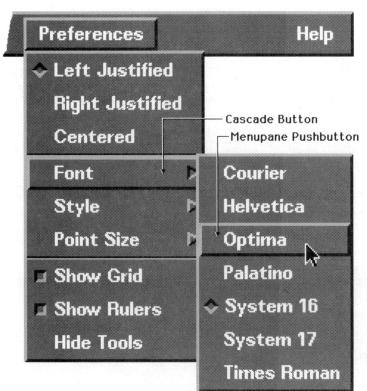

FIGURE 4–55 Cascading Menus are positioned to appear with the first selection of the newly spawned Menupane aligned with the Cascade Button's label.

user must select from a list of alternatives that all pertain to a common topic. For instance, selection of a font size or a color scheme can be best accomplished using an Option Menu. Unlike Radiobuttons, whose selections are viewed all at one time, Option Menus reveal their selections only upon selection. A Menupane pops up from the Option Menu Button when selected. The drawback of using Option Menus is that they cannot be updated dynamically by the end user. As an example, a selection cannot be added to or deleted from an Option Menu's list of choices. The set of choices in an Option Menu must be predetermined and set by the application designer. If a dynamically changing list is desired, a List widget should be used instead. Option Menus can be created using the convenience function **XmCreateOptionMenu.**

The vertical spacing of the children in the MenuPane is specified in the RowColumn resource **XmNspacing.** This value defaults to 1 pixel in the vertical orientation. I recommend that this setting be changed to 0 pixels. This would space the child widgets right above and below one another. This setting will work fine, because the top and bottom shadows of each selection will appear only one at a time upon selection. If necessary, you can change this setting to another specification. Figure 4–56 shows a typical use for Option Menus.

The Option Menu, when spawned from the Option Menu Button, is represented visually as a slab, with each choice represented by a Pushbutton without its Frame. The Pushbutton will display its Frame in the Frame Out position to show that it is the current selection when it has been selected with the mouse. A Label should be associated with an Option Menu button to indicate the topic of the selections in the Option Menu's Menupane. When the user presses on the Option Menu button with the mouse, a Menupane will be spawned, displaying all of the other selections listed in the Menupane, as well as the one displayed in the Option Menu button. A Radiobutton indicator will be shown in its selected state

FIGURE 4–56 Option Menus are used as an alternate method for selecting a "One-of-many" choice.

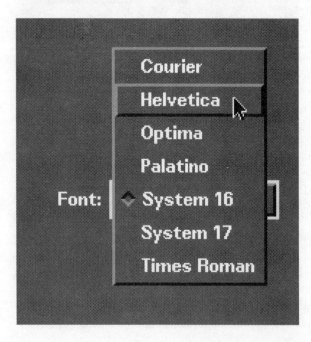

next to the Menu selection that is currently selected and will display it-self in the selected (depressed) state. This Menupane will remain in its popped-up state for as long as the mouse cursor is in the Menupane and the mouse button is pressed. While pressing the mouse button, the user can drag up and down the Menupane, causing each selection to "ripple." This visual feedback to the user is displayed as individual selections pro-truding from the surface, just as Pulldown Menus behave when spawned from a Menubar. When the user releases the mouse button, the new selec-tion will have been made from the Option Menu. The Menupane will un-post itself when the mouse button is released, and the new selection will be displayed on the unselected Option Menu button. Figure 4–57 shows an Option Menu and its spacing and widget components.

Because the selections in the Option Menu's MenuPane involve a "1 of many" selection, a Radiobutton's diamond indicator can be displayed next to the currently selected choice. This keeps the user from having to

FIGURE 4–57 An Option Menu's visual layout components.

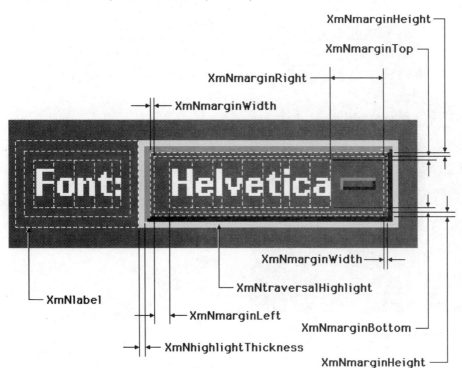

remember the currently selected choice. This is especially helpful in situations where the Option Menu is too close to the top or the bottom of the screen. In these situations, the Menupane will reposition itself to display itself in its entirety by moving over to the side and aligning itself with the bottom or the top. Because of this, the current selection does not always line up with its Label, which can cause the user to lose any visual reference of the current selection. Figure 4–58 shows an Option Menu being repositioned when there is not adequate screen space for its display.

When a number of Option Menus are required to be stacked vertically, they should be lined up along the left edge of the Option Button. When a number of them are required to be lined up with one another horizontally, there should be sufficient space between the Option Menu button of one Option Menu and the Label of the next one. This will prevent them from appearing to run into each other, which could confuse the user as to which Label goes to which Option Menu. Figure 4–59 shows Option Menus in recommended positions for vertical stacking and for horizontal alignment.

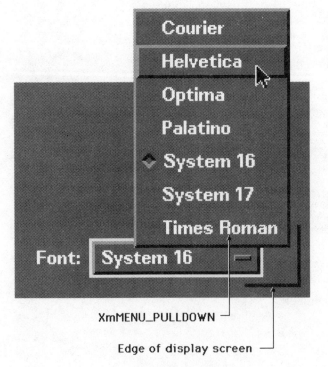

FIGURE 4–58 Option Menus are repositioned when they are forced to be displayed near the edge of the computer display screen.

XmMENU_PULLDOWN

Edge of display screen

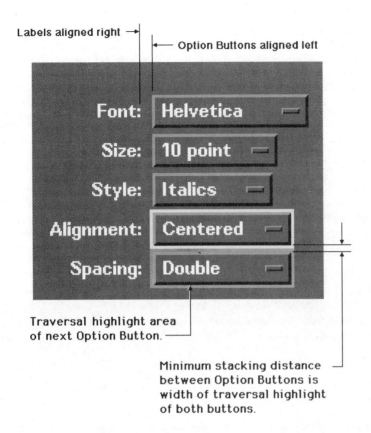

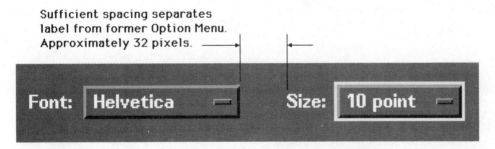

FIGURE 4–59 When stacked, Option Menus should be spaced apart by at least the thickness of their traversal highlights. The space between the Label and its Option Menu button should be aligned when stacked. Labels should be aligned to the right and Option Menu buttons should be aligned to the left. Option Menus laid out in a horizontal row should be spaced far enough apart that the Label of the next Option Menu isn't too close to the previous Option Menu button.

Scrollbars

Scrollbars enable a user to scroll through information in a window. A Scrollbar will allow the user to scroll through information such as listings one line at a time by hitting the arrows at either end, or the user can grab the valuator and run through the displayed items continuously to the end of the document. The user can also click the mouse within the trough area to leap through many lines of information at a time. The valuator indicates the position of the viewer within the document. Its length also represents the size of the portion of the document you are looking at compared with the size of the entire document. For instance, if the valuator fills up the entire channel area, the user is looking at most of the document. However, if the valuator is fairly small, the user is looking at only a small portion of the entire document. Figure 4–60 shows a typical application of Scrollbars.

Scrollbars are represented visually as a varying length valuator within a depressed channel with arrows at either end. Its length and labeling are determined by the software developer and should be set so that the Scrollbar will grow or shrink in length with the resizing of the window manager in which it resides.

Typical Scrollbar

FIGURE 4–60 Scrollbars are typically used for Scrolled Windows.

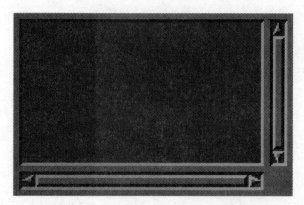

Scrollbars are used with Scrolled Windows

A Scrollbar's colors are assigned in the following manner. The background color is assigned to the top surface of the Scrollbar's valuator. The Scrollbar's top shadow color is assigned to the lower and right chamfer, and the bottom shadow color is assigned to the upper and left chamfer. The valuator's top shadow color is assigned to the left and top chamfer, and its bottom shadow color is assigned to the bottom and right chamfer. Scrollbar's trough color is set automatically to the select color based on the background color. I do not recommend that this color be altered, as the select color helps to emphasize the size of the valuator in the Scrollbar. The select color should be in the Scrollbar trough whether an editable or noneditable window is being scrolled. The Scrollbar's foreground color is ignored because it has no foreground to assign color to.

A Scrollbar's visual dimensions can be specified if its length is not dependent on a resizing manager widget. The width and height of a Scrollbar is specified in the resources **XmNscrollbarWidth** and **XmNscrollbarHeight.** The resource **XmNscrollbarWidth** will always specify the value for a Scrollbar's width (side to side). The resource **XmNscrollbarHeight** will always specify the value for a Scrollbar's height (top to bottom). Remember to reassign the resource values whenever you switch a Scrollbar's orientation. For example, if your Scrollbar is horizontal, **XmNscrollbarWidth** is set to 100, and **XmNscrollbarHeight** is set to 10, the visual result will be a Scrollbar that is 100 pixels long side to side and 10 pixels high. If the Scrollbar's orientation were changed to vertical and these values were not changed, the visual result would be a vertical Scrollbar 100 pixels wide and 10 pixels tall. This will force your Scrollbar to look short and wide. I recommend that the Scrollbar thickness be set to a consistent dimension, whatever the orientation. This can be done by setting the resource **XmNscrollbarHeight** in a horizontally oriented Scrollbar to 16. This will provide a horizontal Scrollbar with a slider height of 8, assuming that the shadow and traversal highlight thicknesses are both set at 2. In the vertical orientation, this same value of 16 would be assigned to **XmNscrollbarWidth.** This will provide a visually slim and ergonomically usable Scrollbar. Figure 4–61 shows a Scrollbar's layout components.

Scrollbars can be oriented either vertically or horizontally. Their maximum height and width values can be specified for each orientation. Scrollbar orientation can be set by specifying one of the following in the resource **XmNorientation:**

XmVERTICAL	This setting orients a Scrollbar to a vertical position.
XmHORIZONTAL	This setting orients a Scrollbar to a horizontal position.

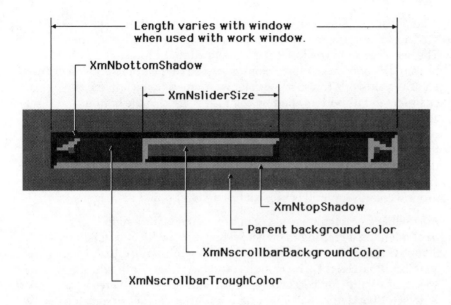

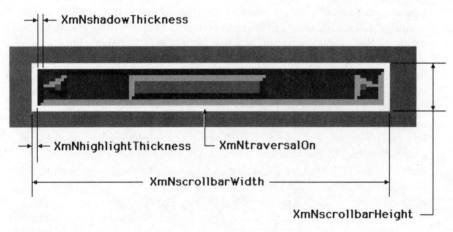

FIGURE 4–61 A Scrollbar's visual layout components.

Figure 4–62 shows a Scrollbar's orientations.

As mentioned earlier, a Scrollbar's valuator indicates the proportion of the document that is being viewed. This applies to both horizontally and vertically oriented Scrollbars. If the valuator extends the entire length of the Scrollbar's trough, the user is viewing the entire length of the document. If the valuator is less than the entire length of the trough, the

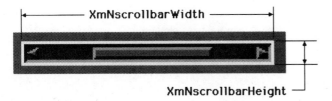

XmNorientation: XmHORIZONTAL

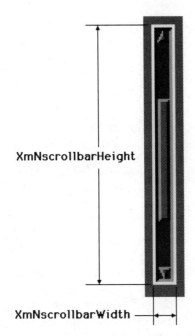

XmNscrollbarWidth ─┤

XmNorientation: XmVERTICAL

FIGURE 4–62 A Scrollbar shown in both horizontal and vertical orientations.

user is viewing a portion of the document equal to the proportion of the valuator realtive to its trough. The position of the valuator within the trough also indicates the area of the document the user is viewing. Figure 4–63 shows examples of the Scrollbar valuator's indication.

Entire
document

Top half of
document

Top fraction
of document

FIGURE 4–63 A Scrollbar's valuator resizes itself as an indication of how much of the entire
document the user is viewing in
the Scrolled Window.

Scrolled Windows

A Scrolled Window creates a window or porthole for viewing a portion
of a much larger document that lies beneath it. A Scrolled Window imple-
ments one or more Scrollbars to enable the user to scroll through the
larger document underneath. The document underneath a Scrolled
Window can contain text or other types of information, such as icons,
drawings, charts, or spreadsheets.

Scrolled Windows are represented visually as a recessed window with
Scrollbars attached along the right and lower sides of the window. A
Scrolled Window should be more than one line in height and should be
as wide as the parent window in which it resides. Scrolled Windows automatically assign the top shadow color to their bottom and right chamfers and the bottom shadow color to their left and top chamfers. The
area within the top and bottom shadows is assigned the background
color. The select color must be assigned manually as the background color
if the Scrolled Window is an editable window. Figure 4–64 shows a typical Scrolled Window.

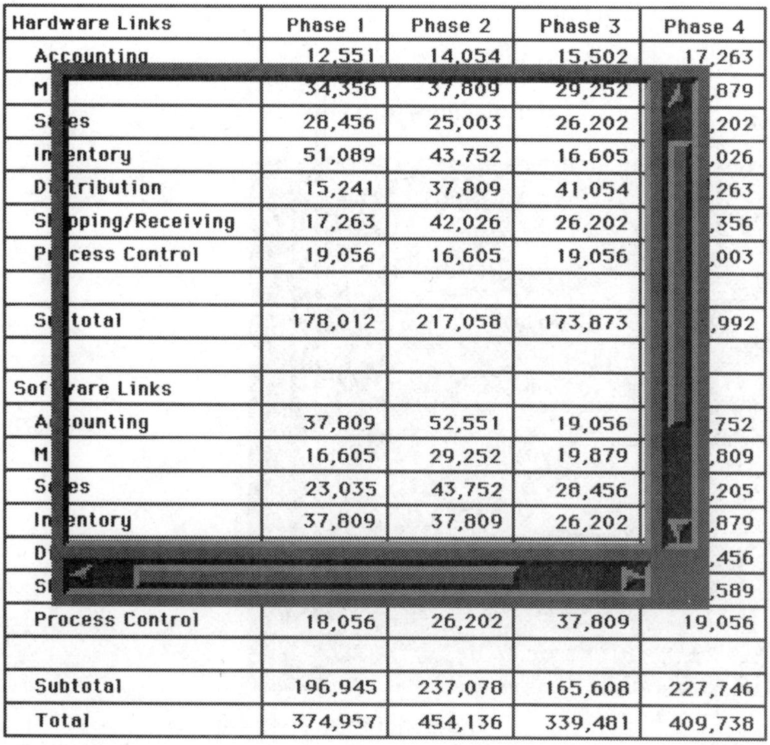

Hardware Links	Phase 1	Phase 2	Phase 3	Phase 4
Accounting	12,551	14,054	15,502	17,263
M	34,356	37,809	29,252	,879
S es	28,456	25,003	26,202	,202
In entory	51,089	43,752	16,605	,026
D tribution	15,241	37,809	41,054	,263
Sh pping/Receiving	17,263	42,026	26,202	,356
Pr cess Control	19,056	16,605	19,056	,003
S total	178,012	217,058	173,873	,992
Sof are Links				
A ounting	37,809	52,551	19,056	,752
M	16,605	29,252	19,879	,809
S es	23,035	43,752	28,456	,205
In entory	37,809	37,809	26,202	,879
D				,456
S				,589
Process Control	18,056	26,202	37,809	19,056
Subtotal	196,945	237,078	165,608	227,746
Total	374,957	454,136	339,481	409,738

FIGURE 4–64 A Scrolled Window is used as a viewport onto the larger document underneath. Its view is changed by scrolling through the document.

A Scrolled Window's Margins

The spacing between a Scrolled Window's borders and its contents is specified in the resources **XmNscrolledWindowMarginHeight** and **XmNscrolledWindowMarginWidth.** Any pixel dimension specified in **XmNscrolledWindowMarginHeight** will be placed between the Scrolled Window's visible contents and its top border and between its visible contents and its bottom border. Any pixel dimension specified in **XmNscrolledWindowMarginWidth** will be placed between the Scrolled Window's visible contents and its left window border and between its visible contents and its right window border. These settings default to 0 and should be left at 0, because it is assumed that the document being scrolled will most likely be larger than the Scrolled Window. This will provide the maximum viewing area in the Scrolled Window without obscuring the document with margins. Figure 4–65 shows the components of a Scrolled Window.

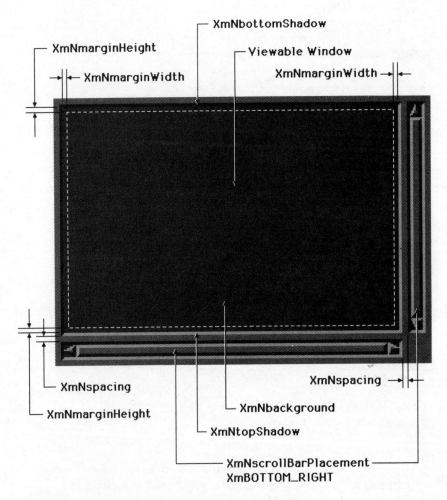

FIGURE 4–65 A Scrolled Window's visual layout components.

A Scrolled
Window's
Scrollbars

A Scrolled Window's Scrollbar behavior can be set in the resource
XmNscrollBarDisplayPolicy. This resource specifies whether the Scrollbar is constantly displayed or whether it appears and disappears
as needed. When this resource is set to **XmAS_NEEDED** and
XmNscrollingPolicy is set to **XmAUTOMATIC**, Scrollbars will appear
only if the viewable window is forced to be smaller than the underlying
data, either vertically or horizontally. When this resource is set to
XmSTATIC, the Scrolled Window will display its Scrollbars regardless

of whether the viewable window is the same size or smaller than the underlying data. I would recommend that this resource be set to **XmSTATIC** whenever a Scrolled Window is used. It would be easier for the user to use an application that is visually stable than to use one whose Scrollbars are constantly being added or deleted while the user is working. By showing the Scrollbars at all times, you let users know that they can scroll past the width or the length of the Scrolled Window and avoid having to guess whether or not the window is scrollable.

Scrollbar Spacing

The Scrollbars are spaced at a certain distance from the Scrolled Window's viewable window. A distance of 4 pixels is set by default in the resource **XmNspacing.** This setting should not be changed, as it provides enough visual separation from the clip area as well as being the minimum dimension that would allow the Scrollbars to display their traversal highlights.

Scrollbar Placement

A Scrolled Window provides four alternative orientations for its Scrollbars in relation to its viewable window. The choice of orientation can be set in the resource **XmNscrollBarPlacement.** The four orientations are as follows:

XmTOP_LEFT	This places the horizontal ScrollBar above the work window and the vertical ScrollBar to the left.
XmBOTTOM_LEFT	This places the horizontal ScrollBar below the work window and the vertical ScrollBar to the left.
XmTOP_RIGHT	This places the horizontal ScrollBar above the work window and the vertical ScrollBar to the right.
XmBOTTOM_RIGHT	This places the horizontal ScrollBar below the work window and the vertical ScrollBar to the right.

Scrollbars should be set in the resource **XmNscrollBarPlacement** as **XmBOTTOM_RIGHT.** This setting will configure the Scrolled Window with the horizontal ScrollBar under the window and the vertical ScrollBar at the right side of the window. This is the location of ScrollBars that is accepted by most users and will be the expected location for Scrolled Windows in most applications. Figure 4–66 shows a Scrolled Window's various Scrollbar orientations.

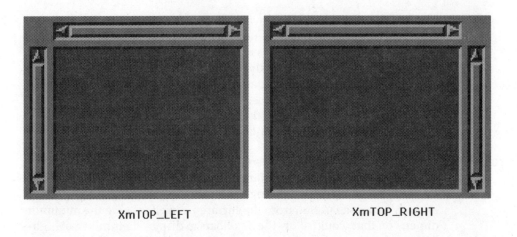

XmTOP_LEFT   XmTOP_RIGHT

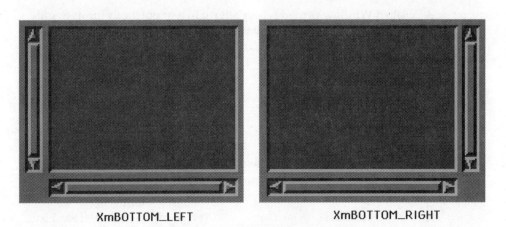

XmBOTTOM_LEFT   XmBOTTOM_RIGHT

FIGURE 4–66 A Scrolled Window's Scrollbars can be configured in four orientations.

Text

Text widgets are used for entering or editing textual or numerical information. A Text widget can be used as a single or multiline text editor for customizing programs or editing document text. Uses for a Text widget can range from single-line text entry, such as filling in forms, to multilined full-page text entry, such as creating a document. This gives the user as well as the application developer a consistent text-editing behavior. A Text widget can be set by the software developer to highlight existing or default text or can be left blank to allow the user to enter data, such as a password. All fonts used in this text area should be the user font, as mentioned in chapter 3. Figure 4–67 shows a typical Text widget.

Text widgets are represented visually as a recessed area filled with text. This recessed area can be set to contain a single line or multiple lines. A single-line Text widget looks like a Pushbutton that has been pressed. This should not confuse the user, because there is never a situation in which a Pushbutton remains depressed. A multiple-line Text widget looks as though an entire region of the panel area has been recessed. The text-editing lines will highlight when they are selected by the mouse or by keyboard.

A Text widget assigns its colors differently than other widgets. It assigns its background color in the recessed area. Its foreground color is used for text. Its Top shadow is the lower and right chamfer, and its bottom shadow is the left and upper chamfer.

A Text widget can be set to be editable or not. An editable Text widget can accept text entry through the keyboard. Editable text should be displayed on a background that is of the select color. This must be specified by the application developer as the Text widget's background color. This slightly darker color will provide a visual cue to the user that this area is editable. A Text widget can be set to editable by setting the resource

Single-Line Text Widget

FIGURE 4–67 A Text widget can be used for display or text entry areas. Single-line text editing widgets should be accompanied by a Label describing the type of information to be entered.

Single-Line Text Widget w/ Label associated with it.

XmNeditable to **True.** Noneditable Text widgets are used for text display only and cannot be edited. To further clarify this distinction, the background of the recessed text area of a noneditable Text widget should be the same color as the parent background. The application developer will not have to specify this, because Text widgets default to the parent's background color. Text widgets can be set to noneditable when the resource **XmNeditable** is set to **False.**

A Text widget's size is affected by the font size that is specified with the widget, as well as by its margin height and width. A Text widget's margin height and width default to 3 pixels. I recommend that the margin height be consistent with the margin height specified in your Pushbuttons. In this way, if both widgets are forced to be positioned next to each other, they will line up correctly. For example, if your Pushbutton margin heights are set to 2, your Text widget's margin height should also be set to 2. This is critical for single-lined Text widgets. Multilined Text widgets should follow this same rule, but it is not as critical, because it is unlikely that other widgets will be horizontally aligned with a multilined Text widget. A Text widget's margin height can be specified in the resource **XmNmarginHeight,** and its margin width can be specified in the resource **XmNmarginWidth.** Figure 4–68 shows a Text widget with all of its widget components.

A Text widget can display either a single line or multiple lines of text. This choice is controlled by the **XmNeditMode** resource, which can be set to the following:

XmSINGLE_LINE_EDIT	This will set the Text widget to be single-lined.
XmMULTI_LINE_EDIT	This will set the Text widget to be multilined.

Figure 4–69 shows an example of a multilined Text widget.

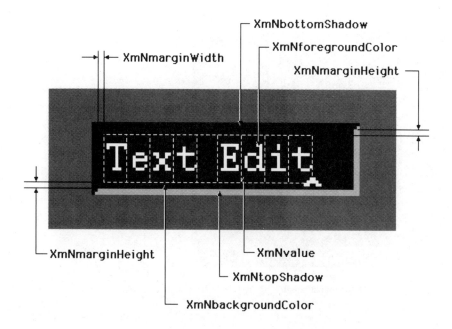

FIGURE 4–68 A Text widget's visual layout components.

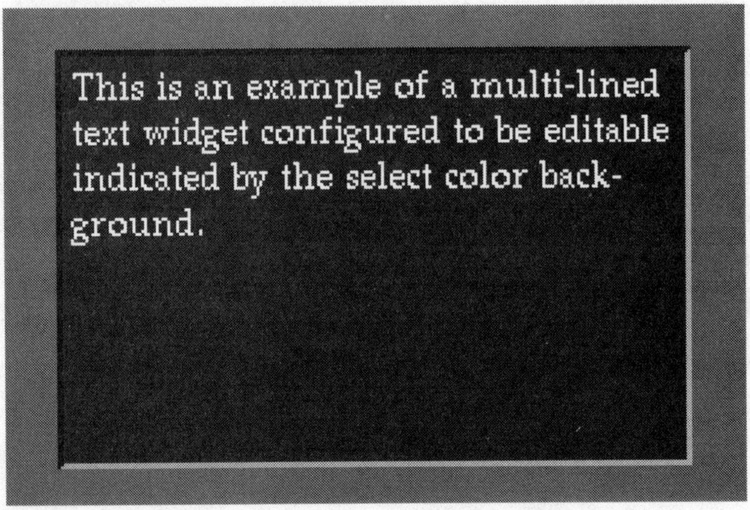

FIGURE 4–69 An example of a multilined Text widget.

Scrolled Text

Text can also be displayed as Scrolled Text. This places the basic Text widget functionality in a Scrolled Window. In this way text that is longer or wider than the viewable area can be scrolled for viewing. This saves space in an often-crowded screen and allows large amounts of text to be viewed in a small space. A Scrolled Text widget can be created with the convenience function **XmCreateScrolledText**. Figure 4–70 shows a typical Scrolled Text window.

A Scrolled Text widget is represented visually as multilined text that can be set to be either display only or editable. It employs a Scrolled Window for its scrolling function. The spacing between the Scrolled Window's borders and its contents are specified in the resources **XmNscrolledWindowMarginHeight** and **XmNscrolledWindowMarginWidth.** Any pixel dimension specified in **XmNscrolledWindowMarginHeight** will be placed between the Scrolled Window's visible contents and its top border and between its visible contents and its bottom border. Any pixel dimension specified in **XmNscrolledWindowMarginWidth** will be placed between the Scrolled Window's visible contents and its left window border and between its visible contents and its right window border. These settings default to 0 and should be changed to 2. This will prevent the text from touching the edge of the Scrolled Text window.

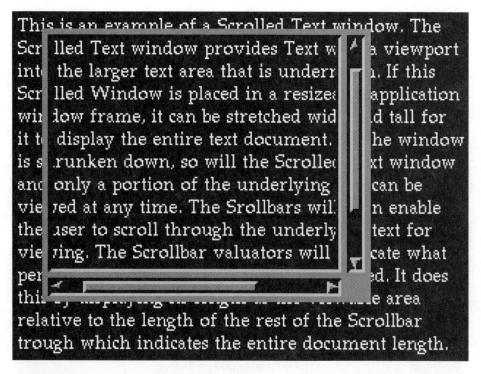

FIGURE 4–70 Scrolled Text windows are Scrolled Windows that are restricted to displaying and editing text.

The number of lines of displayed text can be set in the resource **XmNrows.** This defaults to 1 and is set to a new value automatically when you use **XmNrows.** Motif sets its colors as was described in the previous section on the Text widget. Figure 4–71 shows a Scrolled Text widget with its widget components.

A Scrolled Text widget offers four settings regarding the placement of each Scrollbar:

XmNscrollHorizontal	This adds a Scrollbar horizontally at the bottom of the Scrolled Text window.
XmNscrollLeftSide	This adds a Scrollbar vertically to the left of the Scrolled Text window.
XmNscrollTopSide	This adds a Scrollbar horizontally at the top of the Scrolled Text window.
XmNscrollVertical	This adds a Scrollbar vertically to the right of the Scrolled Text window.

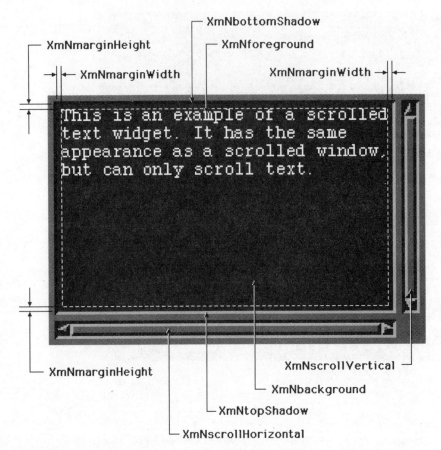

FIGURE 4-71 A Scrolled Text widget's visual layout components.

The *Motif Style Guide* insists that whenever scrolling is provided in a window, the Scrollbars must appear along the right side and along the bottom of the Scrolled Window. Figure 4-72 shows placement of Scrollbars with regard to text.

Accepted Scrolled Text behavior should incorporate word wrap. Word wrap forces lines of text to break between words when text goes off the side of the page. When word wrap is on, horizontal scrolling is not necessary, because text entry will go only as far as the width of the viewable window and will slip to the next line. Word wrap can be turned on by setting the resource **XmNwordWrap** to **True**. This attribute will be ignored if the resource **XmNeditMode** is set to **XmSINGLE_LINE_EDIT**.

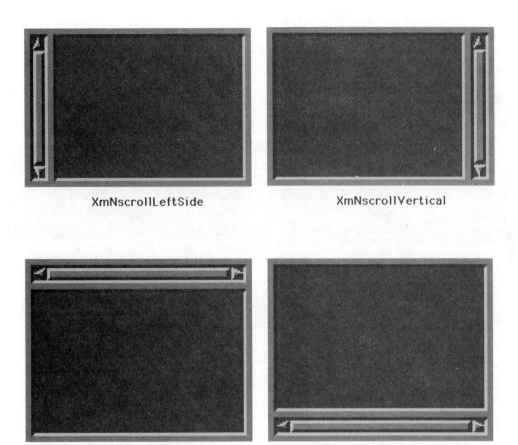

XmNscrollLeftSide   XmNscrollVertical

XmNscrollTopSide   XmNscrollHorizontal

FIGURE 4–72 Scrolled Text Scrollbars can be configured separately.

Scrolled Text widgets can be set to be editable or noneditable in behavior. The color-coding mechanism for editable and noneditable areas should be employed here. If the Scrolled Text widget is noneditable, its background color should be the same as its parent's background color. If, however, the Scrolled Text widget is editable, its background should be set to the select color. The select color, which is slightly darker than the parent background color, will help identify this text area as editable. Figure 4–73 shows a noneditable and an editable Scrolled Text widget with their background colors.

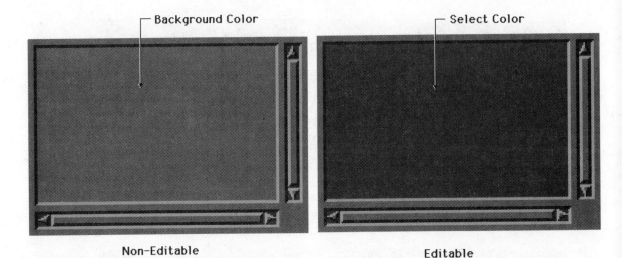

FIGURE 4–73 The background color of noneditable and editable Scrolled Text windows should be colored appropriately. The background color should be used for noneditable Scrolled Text windows, and the select color should be used for editable Scrolled Text windows.

Lists

Users can select one or more items from a List. Items in a List are represented by strings of text. A List widget is useful for creating lists of choices that must have the capability to be changed by the user. Examples of this would be file names, addresses, choices of topics, settings, etc. Text items in a List cannot be edited as they can in Text widgets. Adding or deleting from a List must be done programmatically through other means, such as entry into a dialog box that is programmed to update the current list. Figure 4–74 shows an example of a List.

A List is represented visually as a vertical list of text within a bordered window. Its top shadow color is assigned to the bottom and right chamfers, and its bottom shadow color is assigned to the left and top chamfers. Its background color is assigned to the area within the top and bottom shadows.

FIGURE 4–74 A List is used to display a list of items in a window.

The spacing between strings in a List is determined by the application designer. The strings that are to be displayed as the list items are determined by the setting in the resource **XmNitems**. The total length of the list is specified by the setting in the resource **XmNitemCount.** This number must match **XmNitems** and will be updated automatically by the List widget whenever an item is added to or deleted from the list. The number of items that can be displayed in the List work area, regardless of the entire length of the list, can be specified in the resource **XmNvisibleItemCount.** The displayed portion can be longer or shorter than the actual length of the list. This value will determine the List's visible height.

The spacing between a List's borders and its contents is specified in the resources **XmNlistMarginHeight** and **XmNlistMarginWidth.** Any pixel dimension specified in **XmNlistMarginHeight** will be placed between the List's contents and its top border and between its contents and its bottom border. Any pixel dimension specified in **XmNlistMarginWidth** will be placed between the List's contents and its left border and between its contents and its right border. These settings default to 0 but can be set to any dimension. This dimension should be set to a pixel dimension that provides a minimal margin surrounding the List's items from the window edges. I recommended a dimension of 2 pixels as a minimal margin. Without this margin, the List's items will touch the edge of its display area's beveled edges and will look cramped. Figure 4–75 shows the components of a List widget.

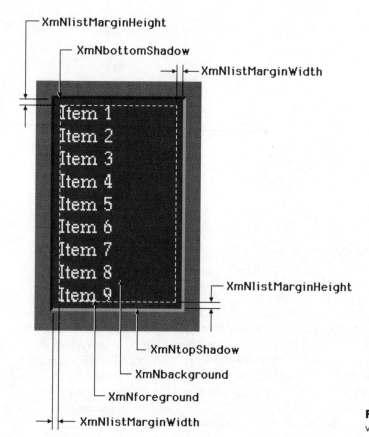

XmNlistMarginHeight

XmNbottomShadow

XmNlistMarginWidth

Item 1
Item 2
Item 3
Item 4
Item 5
Item 6
Item 7
Item 8
Item 9

XmNlistMarginHeight

XmNtopShadow

XmNbackground

XmNforeground

XmNlistMarginWidth

FIGURE 4–75 A List widget's visual layout components.

Scrolled Lists

A Scrolled List allows the user to scroll through items in a list that is longer in length than is possible to display. The Scrolled List acts as a window onto the much longer virtual list that lies underneath. For instance, the user may be looking at a list of 50 items through a Scrolled List that can show only nine items at a time. Most of the resource settings in a Scrolled List are the same as for a List; however, a few additional resource settings must exist. A Scrolled List automatically assumes that you will require a vertical Scrollbar. In a Scrolled List, you can specify a horizontal one as well. Figure 4–76 shows a Scrolled List and how the virtual list can exist under what is viewed.

A Scrolled List incorporates an area of margins that will offset its displayed information from the inside edges of the recessed display window. These margins are placed around the entire list area. The margins

FIGURE 4–76 A Scrolled List allows a list of items to be larger than the amount viewed. The user scrolls through the larger underlying list through the Scrolled List.

between a Scrolled List's borders and its contents are specified in the resources **XmNscrolledWindowMarginHeight** and **XmNscrolledWindowMarginWidth.** Any pixel dimension specified in **XmNscrolledWindowMarginHeight** will be placed between the Scrolled List's visible contents and its top border and between its visible contents and its bottom border. Any pixel dimension specified in **XmNscrolledWindowMarginWidth** will be placed between the Scrolled List's visible contents and its left window border and between its visible contents and its right window border. These settings default to 0. Because the margins for a List should be set at 2 pixels, **XmNscrollWindowMarginHeight** and **XmNscrolledWindowMarginWidth** can be left at 0 pixels.

A Vertical Scrollbar in a Scrolled List

Scrollbars can be set to be added or deleted automatically when the Scrolled List is being used. This behavior can be set in the resource **XmNscrollBarDisplayPolicy.** This resource specifies whether the Scrollbar appears as needed and disappears when not needed. When this resource is set to **XmAS_NEEDED,** the vertical Scrollbar will appear only if the number of items exceeds the visible list. When this resource is set to **XmSTATIC,** the vertical Scrollbar will always be displayed, whether or not the list items extend past the number of list items displayed. I recommend that this resource be set to **XmSTATIC** as often as possible. As was stated earlier regarding the horizontal Scrollbar policy, an application that is visually stable is easier to use than one in which the Scrollbar is constantly added or deleted. Displaying the Scrollbars at all times will indicate that the window is scrollable — and that the user can add an item to the list that is wider than most items in the list or that makes the list longer than can be displayed.

The distance of the Scrollbar from the Scrolled Window in a Scrolled List is specified in the resource **XmNspacing.** This is set to a default of 4 pixels and should not be changed. The default of 4 pixels provides enough visual separation between the Scrolled List's Scrolled Window and its Scrollbars while providing the minimum space requirement for the Scrollbar's traversal highlight if required. Figure 4–77 shows a Scrolled List widget's components.

A Horizontal Scrollbar in a Scrolled List

The presence of a horizontal Scrollbar in a Scrolled List is determined by setting the resource **XmNlistSizePolicy.** This resource will determine whether the list can grow horizontally past the displayed width of the list. If the value in this resource is set to **XmCONSTANT,** the list viewing area will not grow, and a horizontal scrollbar is added automatically. If, however, the resource is set to **XmVARIABLE,** the list will grow to match the size of the longest item, and no horizontal scrollbar will be added. When this resource is set to **XmRESIZE_IF_POSSIBLE,** the Scrolled List will be forced to grow or shrink to match the widest item, and a horizontal scrollbar will appear if the widest item is longer than the displayed list. I recommend that the setting **XmCONSTANT** be employed so that the list window does not grow or shrink before the user's eyes, thus providing a more visually stable scrollable list. It becomes annoying when the window is constantly changing size and when Scrollbars display themselves and undisplay themselves when a new list is brought up. Figure 4–78 shows a Scrolled List with a horizontal Scrollbar.

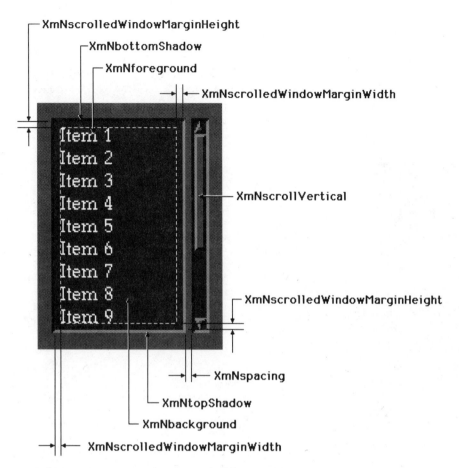

FIGURE 4–77 A Scrolled List widget's visual layout components.

Scrollbars in a Scrolled List can also be positioned by the application developer. A Scrolled List provides four positions for its Scrollbars. Figure 4–79 shows the four possible Scrollbar orientations. These positions can be set in the resource **XmNscrollBarPlacement** as one of the following:

XmTOP_LEFT	This places the horizontal Scrollbar above the list items and the vertical Scrollbar to the left of the list items.
XmBOTTOM_LEFT	This places the horizontal Scrollbar under the list items and the vertical Scrollbar to the left of the list items.
XmTOP_RIGHT	This places the horizontal Scrollbar above the list items and the vertical Scrollbar to the right of the list items.

XmBOTTOM_RIGHT

This places the horizontal Scrollbar under the list items and the vertical Scrollbar to the right of the list items.

I recommend that **XmBOTTOM_RIGHT** be used for all Scrolled Lists. This configuration has been accepted by most users and will be the expected orientation.

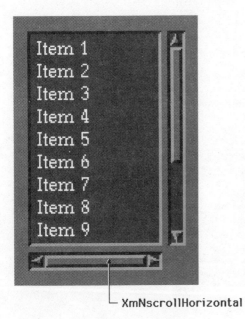

XmNscrollHorizontal

FIGURE 4–78 A Scrolled List can be configured with a horizontal Scrollbar.

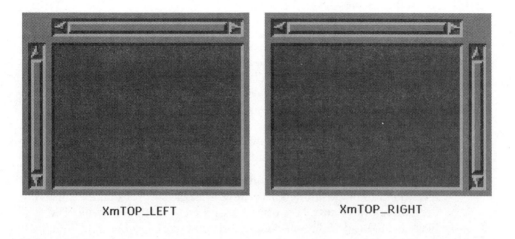

XmTOP_LEFT   XmTOP_RIGHT

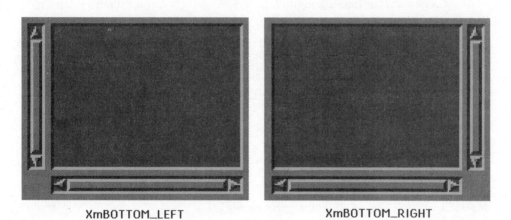

XmBOTTOM_LEFT   XmBOTTOM_RIGHT

FIGURE 4–79 Scrolled List Scrollbars can be configured in four orientations.

The next three container widgets form a predetermined set of constraints that will affect the visual layout of all children and parent
widgets. These widgets are not visible in themselves but do have an
overriding effect on all widgets that are placed within them. These container widgets are complex in their functionality but vital to the layout
configurations of widgets. Entire books can be written describing their
functionality. I will only attempt to describe the visual layout effects
that these container widgets have on primitive and manager widgets.
Refer to the OSF Programmer's Guide or to the numerous other books
written on Motif programming for functional specifications.

Bulletin Boards

The Bulletin Board widget allows you to place your widgets at absolute x and y coordinates. This will also allow overlap of widgets, so be careful in how you place them. The Bulletin Board is the standard container widget used in most dialog boxes, because it allows the most freedom in widget placement. If you have a resizable window frame and your widgets are required to resize with your window, however, this container is not the correct one to use. Because widgets are placed at absolute x,y coordinates, they will remain there and not be allowed to resize themselves.

The Bulletin Board container widget organizes its children freely and allows them to be positioned according to their x,y coordinates. If its children do not have an x,y coordinate assigned to them, they will all be placed at 0,0 and will be stacked up one on top of another. The Bulletin Board widget is the base widget for most dialog boxes and is also used as a general container widget. Figure 4–80 shows how a Bulletin Board arranges its children.

A Bulletin Board can be created from a choice of four styles. The different styles affect the behavioral characteristics of the particular dialog widget. This choice should be specified in the resource **XmNdialogStyle**. The following are the various styles:

FIGURE 4–80 A Bulletin Board diagram shows how it freely arranges its children.

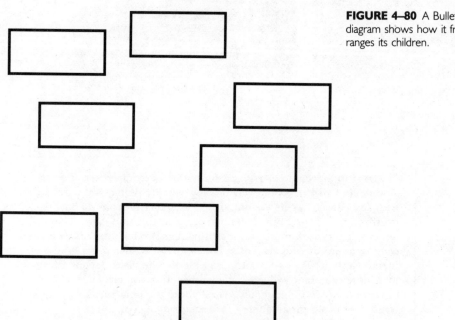

XmDIALOG_SYSTEM_MODAL	This dialog style is used for dialog boxes to which the user must respond before any further interaction can be done in any application in the work environment.
XmDIALOG_APPLICATION_MODAL	This dialog style is used for dialog boxes to which the user must respond before any further interaction can be done in the particular application that produced the dialog box.
XmDIALOG_MODELESS	This dialog style is used for dialog boxes that do not interrupt the use of the application that produced the dialog box. Users can continue to work in the application without responding to the dialog box.
XmDIALOG_WORK_AREA	This dialog style is used for non-dialog-box situations in which a Bulletin-Board-style container widget is required. This style of Bulletin Board is not required to be set in the resource **XmNdialogStyle** and can be used anywhere.

The space between the Bulletin Board's four edges and its children is measured in pixels and can be specified in **XmNmarginHeight and XmNmarginWidth. XmNmarginHeight** specifies the minimum pixel amount of spacing between the top and bottom edges of the Bulletin Board and any child widget. **XmNmarginWidth** specifies the minimum pixel amount of spacing between the left and right edges of the Bulletin Board and any child widget. Motif defaults both of these settings to 10 pixels. You can reset these as desired; however, do not set them to a much smaller value or your child widgets will look too close to the edge. I recommend a distance of 2 pixels for these margin settings. Figure 4–81 shows the appropriate amount of space to assign to a Bulletin Board's margin height and width.

The Bulletin Board can be represented visually in four different styles. These styles determine the look that the Bulletin Board would have within its window manager.

The choice of visual style is specified in the resource **XmNshadowType.** The four choices are as follows:

XmSHADOW_IN	This visual style draws the Bulletin Board as recessed into the surface of the background panel. This is done by drawing the top shadow darker than the background panel and the bottom shadow lighter than the background panel.

XmSHADOW_OUT

This visual style draws the Bulletin Board as raised from the surface of the background panel. This is done by drawing the top shadow lighter than the background panel and the bottom shadow darker than the background panel.

XmSHADOW_ETCHED_IN

This visual style draws the Bulletin Board as etched into the surface of the background panel. This is done by drawing an etched-in double line similar to the Separator as a frame around the Bulletin Board area.

XmSHADOW_ETCHED_OUT

This visual style draws the Bulletin Board as etched-out from the surface of the background panel. This is done by drawing an etched-out double line similar to the Separator as a frame around the Bulletin Board area.

FIGURE 4–81 A Bulletin Board's visual layout components.

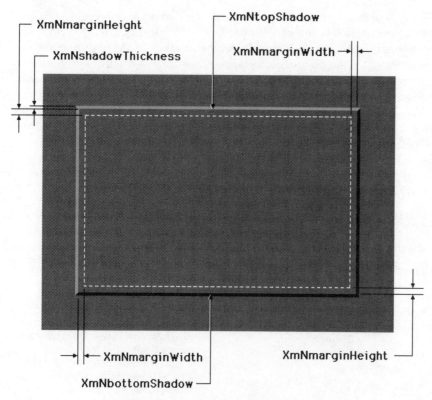

XmNshadowType: XmSHADOW_OUT

Figure 4–82 and 4–83 shows examples of each of a Bulletin Board's various shadow styles.

FIGURE 4–82 Bulletin Boards can be configured with a variety of shadow styles.

XmSHADOW_IN

XmSHADOW_OUT

XmSHADOW_ETCHED_IN

XmSHADOW_ETCHED_OUT

FIGURE 4–83 Bulletin Boards can be configured with a variety of etching styles.

The Bulletin Board container widget is useful for dialog applications in which each child has a different proportion, making the application not conducive to a layout offered using Row/Column or Form. Each child or parent widget in a Bulletin Board is free to be placed wherever the application developer feels is appropriate.

The resizing of a Bulletin Board will also affect the way in which you design your layout. When a Bulletin Board is resized, it does not rearrange its children or parent widgets. It simply crops them if a side is being resized and the widgets no longer fit in their entirety. The resizing characteristic should be specified in the resource **XmNresizePolicy**. Three choices exist for this policy:

XmRESIZE_NONE	This keeps the Bulletin Board in a fixed size, preventing it from being resized.
XmRESIZE_ANY	This allows the Bulletin Board to shrink or grow as needed.
XmRESIZE_GROW	This allows the Bulletin Board to grow as needed but not to shrink past its predesigned layout.

Bulletin Boards also allow you to overlap widgets by setting the **XmNallowOverlap** resource to **True.** I do not recommend this setting; it should be set to **False.** I do not see any occasion in which widgets must be overlapped. Widgets should always be laid out in a manner that gives the users a complete view of them from which to make their selection decisions.

Form

The Form container widget is useful for displaying widgets that must be positioned relative to one another. Forms will allow widgets to resize themselves as their parent window resizes. Widgets in a Form can be placed and sized in relative positions either by percentages or by absolute distances.

The Form container widget organizes its children in positions relative to one another based on the positions assigned to its top, bottom, left, and right sides. Each widget in the Form in essence has a reference widget for each of its four sides. In other words, every widget in a particular Form container widget can refer to its closest widget neighbor and positions itself according that widget's particular Form specifications. For each widget, you can also specify a type of attachment that will define the relationship of that widget to its reference widget. The specifications of the reference widget determine how each of these widgets is positioned, as well as how it is affected when the Form is resized. These attachment specifications are also global settings for every widget in that particular Form; therefore, each widget will position itself consistently to its neighbor widget according to the Form's attachment specifications. Figure 4–84 shows a diagram of a Form with its widgets.

In the Form container widget, every widget is basically affected on its top, bottom, left , and right sides. Each side must be assigned a set of parameters so that each widget will know how to position itself when instantiated and resized. These characteristics will affect each widget's relative position in the Form.

For more technical information about Forms, refer to the *OSF/Motif Programmer's Reference* as well as the *OSF/Motif Application Environment Specifications.*

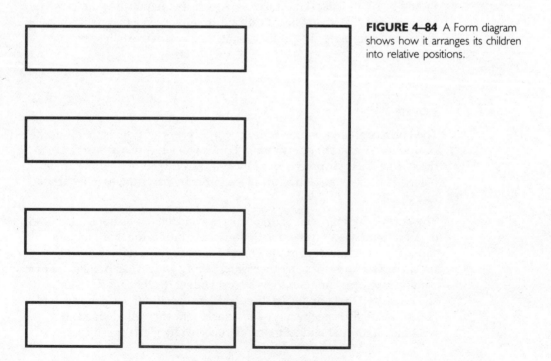

FIGURE 4–84 A Form diagram shows how it arranges its children into relative positions.

RowColumn

The RowColumn container widget is useful for organizing widgets into nice rows and columns. An array of dissimilar-sized Pushbuttons, for example, can be laid out into rows in which each Pushbutton retains its unique size or into columns in which each Pushbutton is forced to a single size.

The RowColumn container widget organizes its children into rows or columns. The **XmRowColumn** resource provides alternate ways in which the RowColumn widget can organize its children. It can organize its children widgets into one or many rows only or into one or many columns only. The number of these rows or columns can be specified in the Row-Column resource file. The orientation of the RowColumn manager can be specified in the resource **XmNorientation.** This resource can be set to columns by specifying **XmVERTICAL** or to rows by specifying **XmHORIZONTAL.**

XmVERTICAL	This setting will set the children into what is called a *column major layout.* This means that all of the children widgets will be organized into vertical columns. The width of the widest widget will be the dimension that will be used for all of the other widgets in that particular RowColumn manager.
XmHORIZONTAL	This setting will set the children into what is called a *row major layout.* This means that all of the children widgets will be organized into horizontal rows. Each widget will have its own dimensions and will not be forced to adopt any other widget's dimensions.

Figure 4–85 shows a RowColumn diagram.

Once the setting of **XmNorientation** is determined, other resource settings must be determined in order to manage the children in this particular layout. The RowColumn widget has a resource called **XmNpacking** that greatly affects the visual behavior of its children. This packing resource will have different effects on the children depending on how the **XmNorientation** was set.

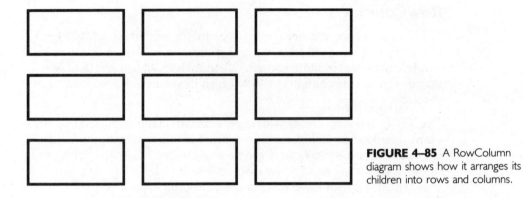

FIGURE 4–85 A RowColumn diagram shows how it arranges its children into rows and columns.

XmPACK_TIGHT	When this is chosen, the children will be packed as tightly as possible, horizontally for RowColumns that are oriented horizontally; vertically for RowColumns that are oriented vertically.
XmPACK_COLUMN	When this is chosen, the children will be resized to match the largest child and placed in an aligned column.
XmPACK_NONE	When this is set, no packing is done and the children will simply stay where they have been assigned according to their x,y coordinates.

Figure 4–86 shows children widgets when placed in rows. Each child retains its individual width.

Figure 4–87 shows children widgets when placed in a column. Each child's width is forced to the width of the widest child.

FIGURE 4–86 A RowColumn organizes its children into rows or columns depending on the packing style specified. This example shows a RowColumn with its children in rows.

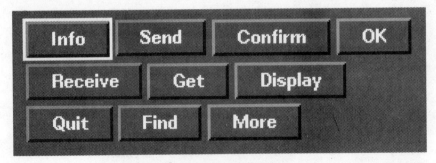

XmNorientation: XmPACK_TIGHT

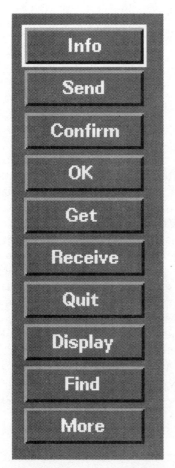

XmNorientation: XmPACK_COLUMN

FIGURE 4–87 A RowColumn organizes its children into rows or columns depending on the packing style specified. This example shows a RowColumn with its children in a column.

The RowColumn widget can specify consistent inner margins for all items contained within it. This is achieved by setting the resource **XmNadjustMargin** to **True.** The values for this margin correspond with the margins in the following widget resources. The inner margins that are adjusted are the top margin **(XmNmarginTop)**, bottom margin **(XmNmarginBottom)**, left margin **(XmNmarginLeft)**, and the right margin **(XmNmarginRight)** of the **XmLabel** inherent in each widget.

When the RowColumn widget is oriented horizontally, **XmNadjustMargin** forces **XmNmarginTop** and **XmNmarginBottom** for all widgets in a particular row to the same value. When the RowColumn widget is oriented vertically, this resource forces **XmNmarginLeft** and **XmNmarginRight** for all widgets in a particular column to the margin values of the widget with the largest margins.

This is a convenient way to ensure that all of your widgets in a RowColumn manager display consistent margins.

A RowColumn widget has features that allow the rightmost or bottommost children to resize themselves with their parent. When the RowColumn is oriented horizontally, when **XmNorientation** is set to **XmHORIZONTAL**, the rightmost of its children are allowed to extend to the edge of the RowColumn manager's right side. This will force the rightmost children to stretch to the rightmost edge of a RowColumn if the RowColumn's parent is stretched to the right or left. When the RowColumn is oriented vertically, **XmNorientation** is set to **XmVERTICAL**, the bottommost of the children widgets are allowed to extend to the edge of the RowColumn manager's bottom side. This will force the bottommost children to stretch to the bottommost edge of the RowColumn if the RowColumn's parent is stretched up or down. These two situations result in visually awkward widget proportions when a RowColumn manager must extend the full length or to the bottom of an application window. I recommend that this not be allowed when using a RowColumn manager. An example of this visually awkward layout is a row of Pushbuttons where the rightmost Pushbutton appears to be considerably longer than the other Pushbuttons just because its RowColumn manager must extend the full width of the application window. This feature can be deactivated by setting the resource **XmNadjustLast** to **False.** Figure 4–88 shows the effect created when the last child is forced to stretch with its RowColumn manager widget.

Widget Dos and Don'ts

Many of the widgets in Motif overlap in their perceived functionality. Although they may look different, from the end user's point of view, some widgets may seem to do the same thing. The decision of which widget to use to do which task rests with the application designer. The choice should be made based on which widget is clearer and easier to manipulate by the end user, not by which is easier to design and program. These decisions must also be based on OSF/Motif-compliant behavior.

For instance, a List widget and an Option Menu look different but can do similar tasks from a user's point of view. On the surface, they both display a list of choices. There are, however, differences in their functionality. The end user can add choices to a List widget. This would be possible

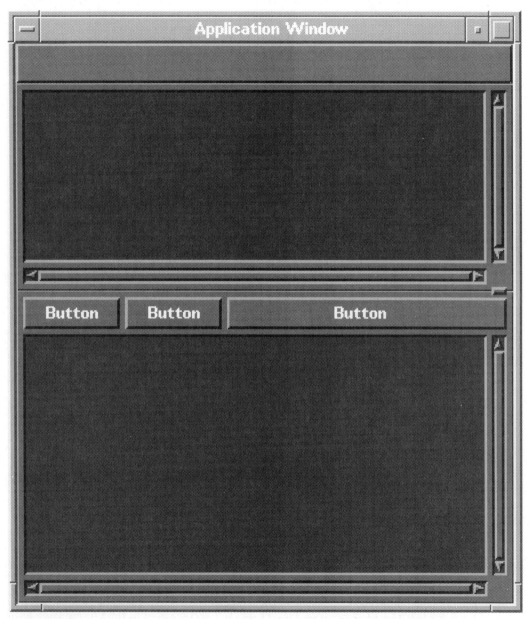

FIGURE 4–88 Do not allow the last child in a RowColumn to stretch and shrink with the application window.

through programmatic means such as through a Command or a Selection dialog box. The end user cannot, however, add choices to an Option Menu. Its selections must be predetermined and set by the application designer.

What are some other differences? Although both display their choices all at once, a List window can be scrollable but takes up more real estate. A List window can be set to various types of selection behavior. An Option Menu takes up much less real estate but allows users to select only one item at a time. A List window can also be set to be editable, so that entries can be added programmatically. An Option Menu cannot be editable by the user. An Option Menu, however, is fast; selection requires about half of the motions it requires in a List window, and the current selection is displayed and refreshed whenever a new selection has been made. You, as the application designer, must decide which is best for the end user.

Another example is Paned Windows and multiple secondary windows. Which is better to use? A Paned Window will divide your application window into several areas, all of which are adjustable in height; however, this flexibility has the drawback that the maximum amount of the application's window cannot be devoted to any one pane. Multiple secondary windows can offer generous real estate to each area; however, the complete context of the application is broken up, which can cause confusion when too many secondary windows are used in any one application.

Should you decide to use a gang of 24 Pushbuttons or should you group them into 4 menu categories each containing 6 selections? Both methods might be effective in invoking an operation, but which would be visually clearer to the end user and allow a minimum number of mistakes?

Early analysis of tasks that the end user would have to go through in using your application will help in determining which widget to select for performing certain tasks. This should be part of the up-front research and analysis of your potential market.

What Not to Do

When designing your application, you should avoid certain configurations for aesthetic reasons, for ergonomic reasons, and because of the difficulty of establishing a work pattern. Here are a few configurations that we have encountered as examples of undesirable widget layout.

Do not gang Pushbuttons in a big group that bombards the end user with a choice of Pushbuttons in multiple rows and multiple columns. Design Pushbuttons into manageable categorized groups that are easy for the user to remember. Once users get accustomed to the layout, they will select from a sense of placement rather than hunting and pecking from a brick wall of Pushbutton choices. Figure 4–89 shows how overwhelming a brick wall of Pushbutton choices can be.

Do not lay out Radiobuttons so that there seems to be an endless list from which to choose. If a list of one-of-many choices becomes quite long, use an Option Menu or a List widget. This will help conserve screen real estate and, more importantly, will be clearer to the end user. Figure 4–90 shows a long list of Radiobuttons that not only looks confusing but is visually unappealing.

Do not label Menu choices with sentences. Use short clear concise words that will convey the operation that the Menu choice will invoke. This also applies to Pushbuttons and Toggles. The longer the widget label, the longer the end user will be forced to read it and the longer it will take to do the task. Long labels as interface choices appear to look like short statements rather than labels. Good examples of short labels are "Print,"

FIGURE 4–89 Do not design overwhelming brick walls of Pushbutton choices.

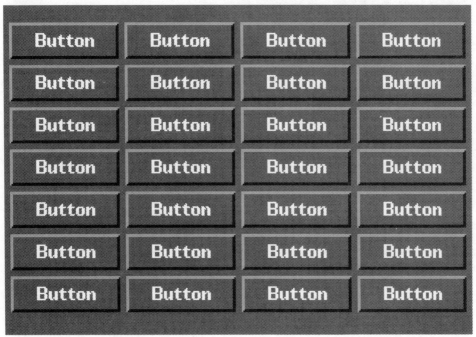

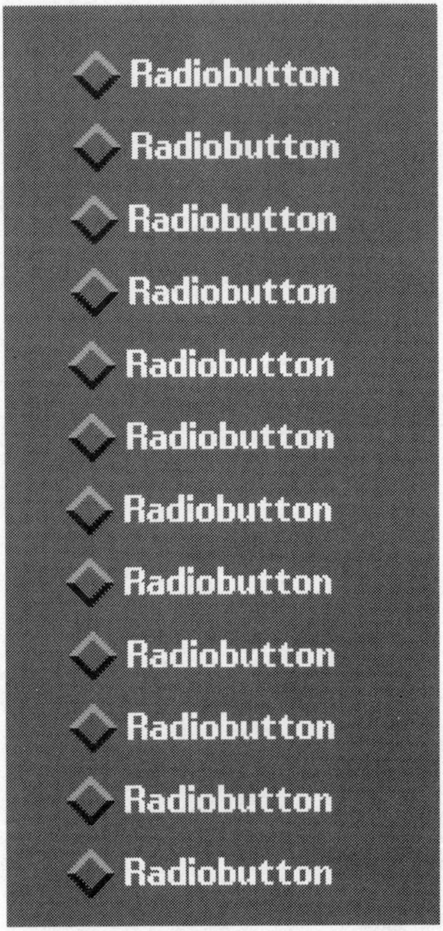

FIGURE 4–90 Do not design long list of Radiobuttons. It not only looks confusing but is visually unappealing and takes up precious screen real estate.

"Save," and "Copy." Bad examples are "Print this to," "Save this document," and "Copy this from" or "Copy this to." It is quite obvious to the end user that a selected action will be performed on the document. These choices should be brief and to the point and should not waste the user's time. Figure 4–91 shows that a Menupane with long multiple word selections is not as clear and concise as one with short commands.

Do not use varying sizes or styles of fonts in designing the interface of your application. Though it may sound fun and whizzy to have fonts of varying sizes and styles, the results are often gaudy and do nothing to help present the interface to the end user. The use of varying sizes and styles also disrupts the sizing of the widgets. Because the sizes of widgets are based on the font size, varying font sizes can result in varying sizes

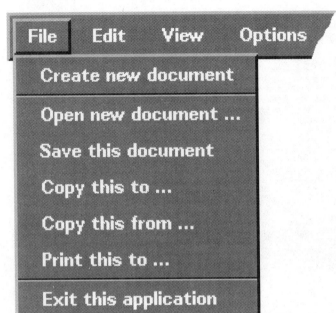

FIGURE 4–91 Do not design Menupanes with long multiple-word selections. They are not as clear and concise as short commands.

of widgets. Varying styles can also lead to varying usage of the space available. Some fonts require more space than others, thus leading to an inconsistency in spacing. After a while, the end user develops a physical pattern of movement, expecting the MenuPulldowns to be of a certain length as well as expecting Pushbuttons to be a certain height and width. Varying sizes and styles of fonts will cause inconsistencies that a user may never get used to. Use consistent fonts and save the glitz for the application work area in creating WYSIWYG and DTP documents. Figure 4–92 shows how varying the font style within an application does nothing to enhance the interface.

Do not use widgets for functions other than those they were intended for. For example, do not switch functional attributes between widgets, such as spawning an Option Menu from a Text edit widget, or spawning a Cascading Menu from a Pushbutton. The users of Motif will expect consistency in behavior from these widgets in varying applications and will be surprised when a widget does not behave in a predictable manner. It

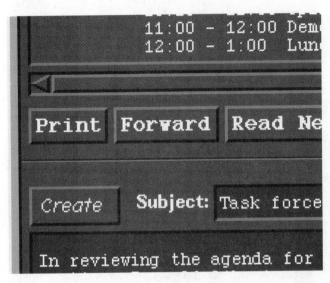

FIGURE 4–92 Do not use varying font styles within an application. They do nothing to enhance the interface.

is best to keep the functionality of the widgets you use as nearly OSF/Motif-compliant as possible. Figure 4–93 shows an example of using widgets for functions other than those they were intended for.

Do not display one-of-many choices represented with Radiobutton diamond indications in a Scrolled List. Use the proper selection mechanism when using a Scrolled List. Though using a Scrolled List conserves vertical screen real estate, widgets such as Radiobuttons or any other widget should not be scrolled. A Scrolled List should contain only text that represents choices. Radiobuttons or other widgets should be displayed on the background surface of the application or dialog box. Figure 4–94 shows an inappropriate use of Radiobuttons in a Scrolled List.

If the Menubar is shortened to a length shorter than the minimum length of all of the Menu selections usually in a resizeable window manager, it will wrap and create a second row for the Menu selections that were cut off. **Do not** resort to multiple row Menubars. This not only looks awkward, but also takes up vertical space in your application window and covers up other Menubar selections when an upper row selection is being made. Plan your design so that Menubar selections have labels that are as short and succinct as possible. In this way, if a user were to resize the

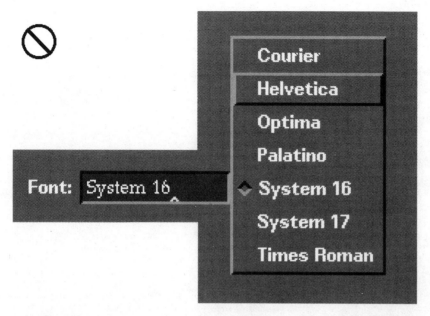

FIGURE 4–93 Do not use widgets for functions other than those for which they were intended. This example shows a Menupane spawned from a Text widget. This breaks the model already established for Text widgets and Menupanes.

application window to the narrowest workable size, the Menubar would still be displayed as one row of selections. Figure 4–95 shows a Menubar when it is forced to a double row.

Do not use multiple words as Menubar topics. Each topic in the Menubar should be a single word. Multiple-word topics are discouraged because they tend to confuse the user and because they take up too much horizontal space and look awkward. Keep your topics short, succinct, and as single words. Figure 4–96 shows how multiple-word topics can lead to confusion and clutter in the application.

Do not end the separation short of the edges. When displaying Separators, make sure that the etched separation line extends across and to the very end of the area that is separated. This will not give as convincing a look of separation as if it extended completely. To set the Separator to extend to the end of its widget, set the resource **XmNmargin** to 0. Figure 4–97 shows the correct separation distance.

FIGURE 4–94 Do not design Radiobuttons in a Scrolled List. It is inappropriate to scroll through widgets. Only data should be scrolled.

Do not allow any rows of widgets to be clipped when the Panes are re-adjusted when using Paned Windows in an application. Any row or inter-face components should be configured so that they cannot accidentally obscure any functionality. Figure 4–98 shows a row of Pushbuttons clipped from an adjustment of the Paned Window.

Do not allow widgets to be clipped when the size of an application's window frame is adjusted. A minimum width should be established so that the window frame can be shrunk to a limit. Figure 4–99 shows widgets be-ing clipped by readjustment of an application's window frame.

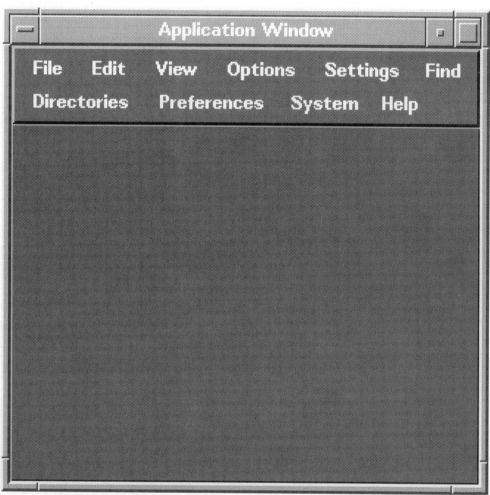

FIGURE 4–95 Do not design Menubars that are forced into a double row because of a lengthy number of topics. Keep the number of topics down so that the Menubar can display itself as a single row.

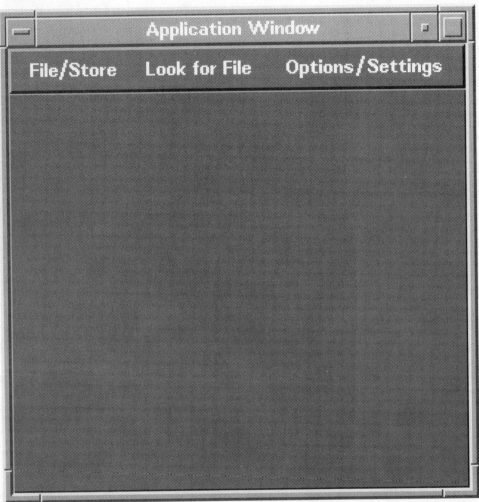

FIGURE 4–96 Do not use multiple word topics in Menubars. This can lead to confusion and clutter in the application.

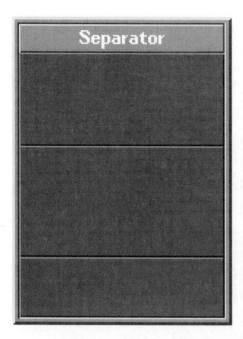

Separators should extend
to edges of area.

Do not stop Separators short of
edge of area.

FIGURE 4–97 Do not specify Separators to stop short of the edges of an application work area. Specify Separators to extend to the very edges of a work area.

FIGURE 4–98 Do not allow a row of Pushbuttons or other widgets to be clipped from an adjustment of the Paned Window.

FIGURE B–1 The Dashboard designed for HP VUE contains a cohesive unit of frequently used functions, which previously were scattered throughout the screen. This integrated format helps the user to easily remember where each function is located, and it cuts down the effort required to constantly look for a particular tool. Access to each of the six workspaces provided in HP VUE 2.0 also can be obtained through the Dashboard.

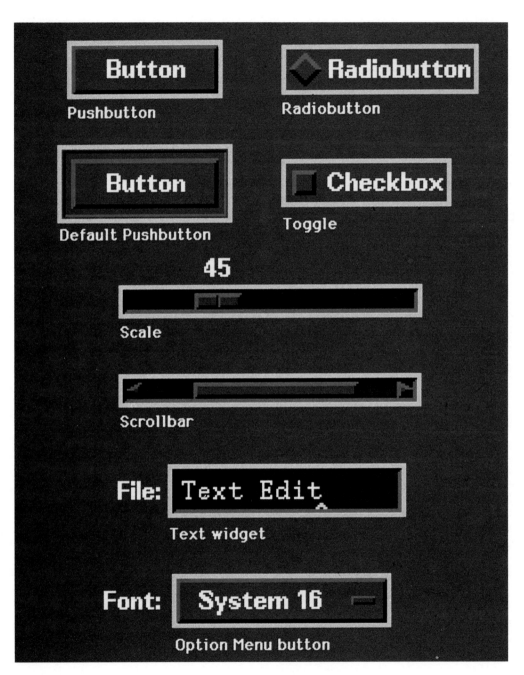

FIGURE B–2 Various Motif widgets with their traversal highlight displayed.

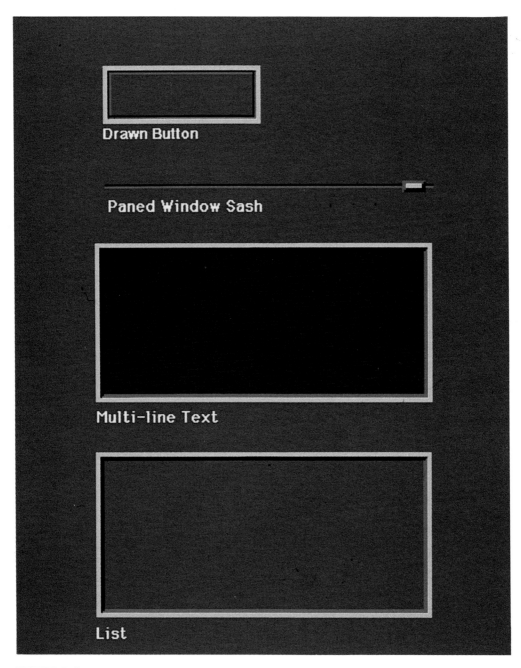

FIGURE B–3 Various Motif widgets with their traversal highlight displayed.

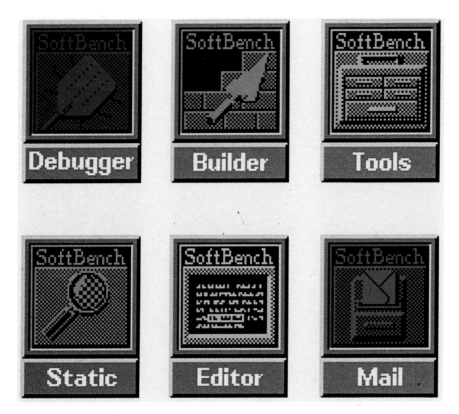

FIGURE B-4 Examples of minimized icons used in HP SoftBench suite of Computer Aided Software Engineering (CASE) tools. A dithering technique was used to design these icons in order to convey a three-dimensional appearance while being restricted to only two colors. Whimsical, visual metaphors are often used when the function cannot be literally represented.

FIGURE B–5 Examples of manipulable icons designed for HP VUE 2.0 File Manager. These icons represent directories, files, and executable files, and they are manipulable with a proprietary drag and drop functionality.

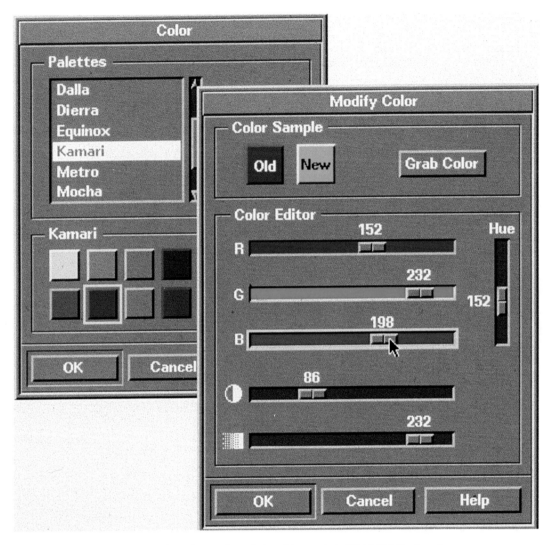

FIGURE B-6 Dialog Boxes, such as these color palette editing tools in HP VUE 2.0, allow the user to quickly manipulate his/her screen environment without understanding how to configure the X defaults.

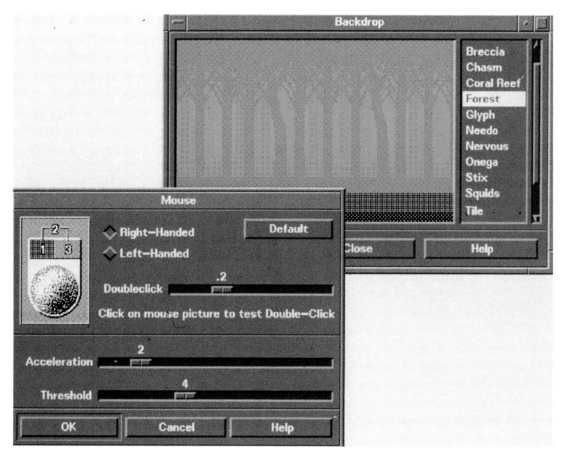

FIGURE B-7 Opportunities for dialog box design are many. These two from HP VUE 2.0 allow the user to change background patterns and reconfigure mouse attributes.

FIGURE B–8 The Style Manager tool in HP VUE 2.0 is represented as a bar of Pushbuttons with icons and labels. The combination of icons and labels help the user to quickly recognize the desired functionality.

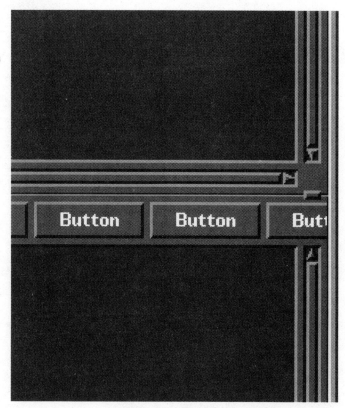

FIGURE 4–99 Do not allow widgets to be clipped by a readjustment of the application's window frame.

Motif's Window Manager

5

Chapter

Motif provides a Window Manager that allows your applications to be manipulated directly on the display screen. The Window Manager provides essential functions that make using applications easy and convenient for the user by allowing applications to be displayed in window frames. The user can manipulate the window frames directly by using the mouse. The window frame that is the visual representation of the Window Manager can be turned on or off. Whether it is turned on or off, your applications will still be displayed on the screen; however, if the window frame is turned off, the visual cues for direct manipulation of window operations are removed. In this case, a combination of keystrokes and/or mouse buttons must be used to allow the user to move or resize the window.

Motif provides a window frame that can be configured in a variety of ways. This window frame can be configured for use in application windows as well as for dialog boxes and icons. It can be configured with resizable or nonresizable borders. The user can manipulate a window's size directly in the resizable version simply by selecting and moving any of the borders while keeping the mouse button pressed. The window frame can also be configured with different Titlebars. The Titlebar options are Titlebar only, Titlebar with Minimize, or Titlebar with Maximize and Minimize. The Maximize button allows the application to expand to be as large as possible, often filling the entire computer screen. The Minimize button allows the window to shrink into an icon without shutting down the application. The Titlebar allows the window to be moved by direct manipulation using the mouse. Selecting and holding down on the Titlebar with the mouse button pressed allows the user to move the window anywhere on the screen simply by moving the mouse.

The visual representation of the window frame is completely three-dimensional. It requires only top shadow, background, and bottom shadow values as its color set. It does not require the slightly darker select color, because there is no need to show depression or editability on a window frame. This means that only three colors are required for a Window Manager color set, compared to the four required for a widget or a gadget. The Window Manager does, however, require another set of three colors to show its state change when it changes its active input focus. You should be prepared to set aside six color cells in the system color map for the Window Manager color sets. The window frame's foreground color, like that of widgets, is flipped between black and white automatically.

Active Input Focus

With the number of overlapping windows increasing on the user's screen, the active input focus color helps the user to identify which window is connected to the keyboard. When an application has the input focus, it will receive keystrokes to the exclusion of other windows. Motif provides a visual state change by changing the color of the window frame of the application or dialog box that receives the active input focus.

The active input focus can be set to react either explicitly or implicitly. If it is set to react explicitly, the window gets the input focus only when the mouse button is pressed when the pointer is within the application window. If it is set to react implicitly, the window gets the input focus when the user simply moves the mouse pointer into the window — users do not have to click in the window. As the mouse pointer enters into one window from another, the colors of the window frame that is entered will change to the active input colors. In implicit mode this will happen as the mouse enters the new window. In explicit mode, this will happen as the mouse is clicked in the new window. The colors of the window the mouse pointer is leaving will change into the window frame colors shared by all the other window frames on the screen in implicit mode. In explicit mode, this will happen as soon as the mouse is clicked in a new window.

The color that is used as the active input focus color of the window frame should be a bright and somewhat saturated color, and the inactive input window frames should be a subdued color. These colors should harmonize well together while being different enough in brightness or saturation that the active input focus color will get the user's attention. Figure A–8 (in the color section earlier in this book) shows how the active input focus color distinguishes itself from the other windows.

The window frame color must be specified for both the active state (the state of the window that has the input focus) and the inactive state (the state of the window that does not have the input focus). This color can be specified in the resources **Mwm*background** and **Mwm*activebackground**. In most cases, only the background color needs to be specified; the top and bottom shadow colors as well as the foreground color will be generated automatically.

If, however, you want to configure all of the appearance details of the window frame manually, the following resources will have to be specified in addition to the ones mentioned above. The following resources must be specified if you want to set individually each color and pixmap pattern in an inactive window frame.

> **Mwm*foreground**
>
> **Mwm*topShadowColor**
>
> **Mwm*bottomShadowColor**
>
> **Mwm*topShadowPixmap**
>
> **Mwm*bottomShadowPixmap**
>
> **Mwm*backgroundPixmap**

The following resources must be specified if you want to set individually each color and pixmap pattern in an active window frame.

> **Mwm*activeForeground**
>
> **Mwm*activeTopShadowColor**
>
> **Mwm*activeBottomShadowColor**
>
> **Mwm*activeTopShadowPixmap**
>
> **Mwm*activeBottomShadowPixmap**
>
> **Mwm*activeBackgroundPixmap**

Window Frames

The window frame can be created as a resizable or a nonresizable border. Resizable window frames can be resized from any of the four sides or corners to any size that the user desires. To do this, the user would simply grab hold of any of the window frame resize borders by pressing the mouse button with the pointer on the desired border; the user would then move the mouse as desired for a new window size. The window frame border width should be wide enough that the user can easily place the mouse pointer to grab hold of the resize border. This width should not, however, be so wide that the window manager borders look thick and heavy. Resizable window frames should be used on application windows as well as secondary windows and dialog boxes that require resizing during their use. Figure 5–1 shows a typical resizable window frame.

Nonresizable window frames cannot be resized directly by holding the mouse button down and grabbing a border. Because the nonresizable window frames cannot be grabbed by the mouse pointer and moved, the border width of the nonresizable window frame should be as thin as possible to minimize the screen real estate required. The borders should, however, be wide enough to provide a visual indication of input focus. They should be used on secondary windows and dialog boxes that do not require resizing during their use. Figure 5–2 shows a typical nonresizable window frame.

The thickness of the window border for resizable and nonresizable windows can be specified in the following resources:

Mwm*resizeBorderWidth	This resource specifies the width of the border with resize borders.
Mwm*frameBorderWidth	This resource specifies the width of the border without resize borders.

The width specified for the Window Frame includes the top and bottom shadows as well as the flat background area. All top and bottom shadow widths are 2 pixels regardless of the frame width dimension. This dimension cannot be changed. The default values for the widths of the two frame styles in Motif are as follows:

> **Mwm*resizeBorderWidth: 10**
>
> **Mwm*frameBorderWidth: 5**

Application windows are already suffering from the need to maximize their screen real estate and minimize their visual detail. The resizable window frames that are typically used as application window frames default to 10 and can benefit from a thinner width. A value of 7 is

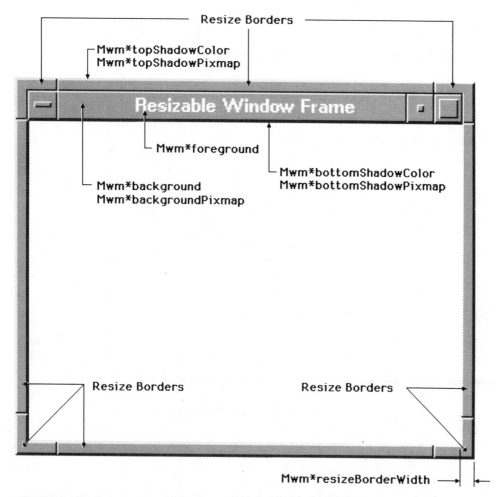

FIGURE 5-1 A typical resizable window frame with its components.

recommended for minimizing the visual bulk of the window frame while keeping it wide enough that a user can grab hold of it with the mouse pointer. Figure 5–3 shows a more appealing dimension for resizable window frames.

Dialog boxes are usually designed using nonresizable window borders. On occasion, they are found to have resizable window frames. The nonresizable window frames used with dialog boxes default to 5. This width is fine for a window border that does not require any resizing with the mouse; however, a width of 5 allows a background width of only 1 pixel in the window frame. This is not enough area for the active input focus

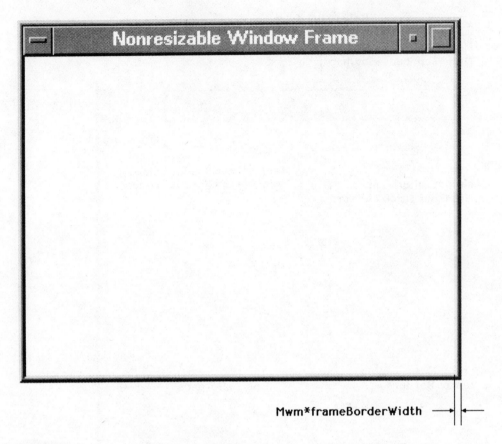

FIGURE 5–2 A typical nonresizable window frame.

color to show well. I recommend that this be increased to from 5 to 6. This will create a 2-pixel background width and will double the active input focus color area while increasing the border width by only 1 pixel. Figure 5–4 shows a nonresizable window frame increased by 1 pixel.

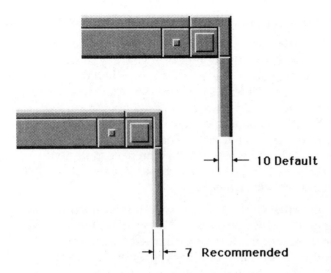

10 Default

7 Recommended

Mwm*resizeBorderWidth

FIGURE 5–3 Motif defaults the resizable window frame width to 10. A more appealing width would be 7, which displays a thinner window border while allowing enough visual width for grabbing with a mouse pointer.

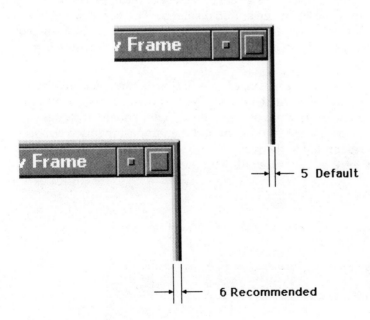

5 Default

6 Recommended

Mwm*frameBorderWidth

FIGURE 5–4 Motif defaults the nonresizable window frame width to 5. This provides a 1-pixel window frame background, which is too thin for displaying the active input focus color. A width of 6 would provide a better visual indication of the active input color while not drastically increasing the border width.

Titlebars and Maximize and Minimize Buttons

The Titlebar displays the title of the application or dialog box, as well as allowing the user to move the application or dialog box by simply moving the mouse while holding down the mouse button when the mouse pointer is on the Titlebar. The Titlebar's top and bottom shadows reverse to show that it is being selected. The background color of the Titlebar does not darken as it does in Pushbuttons and Toggles. Titlebars incorporate Labels for use as their application titles. The font used in the Label should be consistent in style and size with other interface fonts used throughout the application. This will ensure a cohesive look to the application. Figure 5–5 shows a typical Titlebar.

On the right side of the Titlebar, the Maximize and Minimize buttons are located. These buttons allow the application window to be either maximized to fill the entire computer screen or minimized into an icon while allowing the application to continue running. These buttons can be set so that they appear as Minimize, Maximize and Minimize, or no function at all. There are situations in which any of the three are appropriate.

Primary or main application window frames should have the Maximize and Minimize buttons displayed. Figure 5–6 shows the Maximize and Minimize buttons in a window frame.

Secondary windows that are essential to the use of the application should have only the Minimize button displayed. There should not be any need to maximize a secondary window; they should not be designed to warrant being that large. Figure 5–7 shows the Minimize button in a window frame.

Most dialog boxes, such as message boxes or state-setting dialog boxes, should not display any of these buttons. There should be no need to maximize or minimize these types of dialog boxes. They should be designed to display a message or a state change and then unpost themselves once the user has responded to them. Figure 5–8 shows a window frame with no Maximize or Minimize button in the Window Manager.

FIGURE 5–5 A typical Titlebar in a window frame includes the window title, Maximize and Minimize buttons, and the window menu button.

Maximizes Application Window ⎯

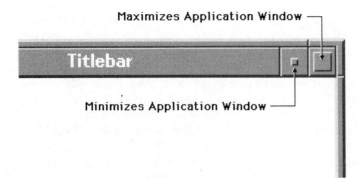

Minimizes Application Window ⎯

FIGURE 5–6 The Maximize and Minimize buttons on a window frame allow the user to either maximize (enlarge) the window to fill the display screen or minimize (shrink) the window into an icon.

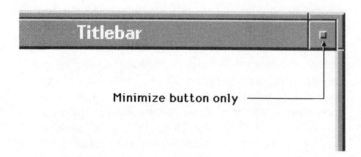

Minimize button only ⎯

FIGURE 5–7 Window frames can be configured to display only the Minimize button.

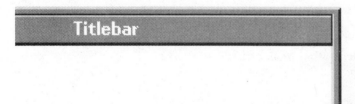

FIGURE 5–8 Window frames can be configured not to display a Maximize or a Minimize button. This is usually the case with dialog boxes.

Window Menus

The Window Menu is used for choices that affect the application window. It can be selected by pressing on the square button in the upper left hand corner of the window frame with the mouse pointer. Figure 5–9 shows the window menu button.

When the user selects the window menu button, the window Pulldown Menu is displayed. It usually contains choices such as Move, Close, etc. By default, the window menu is assigned the same color as the inactive input focus color. Therefore, when an application is operating, although the window frame will display the active input focus color, the window menu will display the inactive input focus color. As an option, the window Pulldown Menu color can be changed in the resource **Mwm*menu*background**. An alternative color for the window Pulldown Menu is the active input focus color. This would match the active window frame color. There are benefits and drawbacks to this. The benefit is that the window Pulldown Menu will match the active input focus color of the window with the input focus. This will show visual consistency between the window frame and its Pulldown Menu, because the active input color will be shown when this Pulldown Menu is selected. The drawback would be a harsh color combination depending on the color used. Figure 5–10 shows a typical window Menupane.

The configuration of the window frame for primary windows can be specified in the resource **Mwm*clientDecoration**. The configuration of the window frame for secondary windows can be specified in the resource **Mwm*transientDecoration**. Motif provides a variety of preconfigured values that can be specified in this resource. These values are considereddaditive if preceded by a plus sign (or a blank). They are considered subtractive if preceded by a minus sign. For example, to remove the Maximize button from all primary windows, you would use the following:

Mwm*clientDecoration: -maximize

or

Mwm*clientDecoration: resize menu minimize

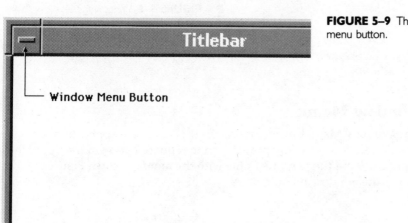

FIGURE 5–9 The window menu button.

Window Menu Button

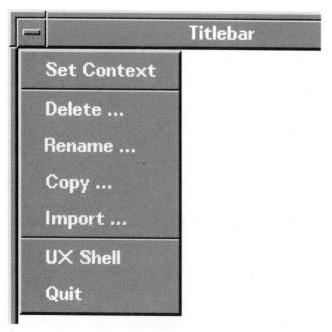

FIGURE 5–10 The window Menupane.

The following values are provided by Motif (note that "menu," "minimize," and "maximize," imply "title"):

all	Provides a fully decorated window frame complete with resize borders and a Titlebar with Minimize and Maximize buttons.
none	Provides no visible window frame.
border	Provides a window frame border with no resize handles.
resizeh	Provides a window frame border with resize handles.
title	Provides a title with text only.
titlebar	Provides a title with window menu and Minimize and Maximize buttons.
minimize	Provides the Minimize button.
maximize	Provides the Maximize button.
menu	Provides the window menu button.

The client Decoration resource can be set on a per-application basis. As an example, to put only a small border around xload windows, you would use the following:

Mwm*xload*clientDecoration: border

The transient Decoration resource, by comparison, can be set only globally, not for individual windows.

Mattes

Mattes are used to provide a distinguishing colored inner frame for clients without interfering with the active and inactive coloring of the regular window frames. Mattes are controlled by the Window Manager but can be activated and colored on a per-application basis. Mattes appear as frames that wrap themselves around the center bitmap. The overall size of a frame with a Matte depends on the dimensions of the bitmap that is being wrapped by the Matte. Figure 5–11 shows a window with a Matte.

FIGURE 5–11 Mattes can be placed within a window frame to any width.

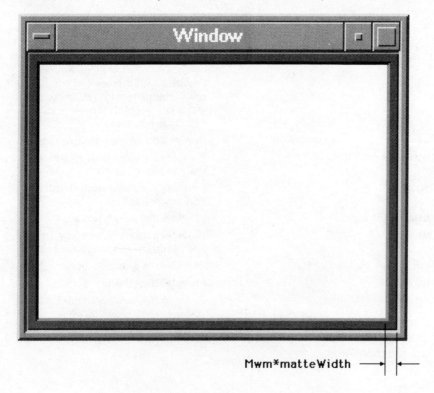

When specifying Mattes, you must specify the pixel dimensions as well
as the background color. The pixel dimension includes the top and bottom shadows as well as the background. For example, a dimension of 8
pixels will provide a Matte with a 2-pixel-wide top shadow, a 2-pixel-
wide bottom shadow, and a 4-pixel-wide background. The size of Mattes
for primary and secondary windows can be specified in the resource
Mwm*matteWidth. The color of the Matte's background can be specifie-
din the resource **Mwm*matteBackground.** When specifying these resources, you normally include the client name. For example, suppose you
wanted your bitmapped image window to have a Matte. You would
specify both the **MatteWidth** resource with a positive value and the
MatteBackground resource with a color of your choice:

Mwm*name*matteWidth: **8**
Mwm*name*matteBackground: **turquoise**

This would give you a turquoise Matte that is 8 pixels wide. This value includes the Matte's top and bottom shadows. By default, applications
have a **MatteWidth** of 0. Figure 5–12 shows a nonresizable window with
a Matte and its visual components.

Normally, the shadows are generated automatically based on the background color. However, if you want to configure the shadows, the following resources will have to be specified.

    Mwm*matteTopShadowColor

    Mwm*matteTopShadowPixmap

    Mwm*matteBottomShadowColor

    Mwm*matteBottomShadowPixmap

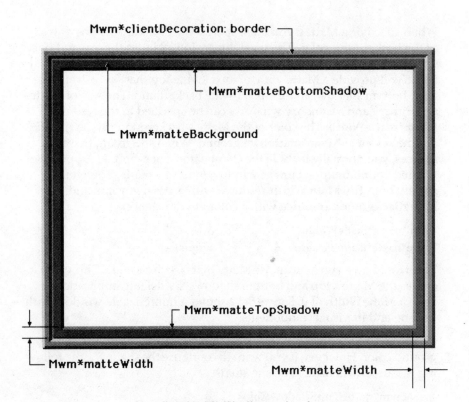

FIGURE 5–12 A Matte's visual components.

Icons

6

Chapter

For anyone who is involved in developing, using, or understanding graphical user interfaces, the word *icon* conjures up many varying images. Icons are typically thought of as graphical images that represent an application or document that is either idle (shut down and not running) or minimized (visually miniaturized and running). Icons can also be thought of as symbols that express a function, such as the icon symbols of the standard dialog boxes that are provided with Motif. Icons can also be symbols that represent a function in lieu of a Label. These types of symbols can be used instead of words on widgets such as Pushbuttons. This would help reduce the problem of internationalization. Industrial designers have used this symbolic labeling for decades in products from automobile dashboard controls to toasters.

Icons can also be a great way to save precious screen real estate and can be helpful in designing consistently dimensioned controls if necessary. They are great for conveying a lot of information in a small amount of space.

What Are Icons?

There is beginning to be great confusion in the GUI world as to a clear definition of an icon. The distinction of what is an icon and what is not is becoming grayer every day. Although restraint should be exercised with regard to the number and types of icons used, application developers have a great desire to use more icons in order to make their applications seemingly easier to understand.

By definition, an icon is a bitmapped image that represents an application or a document. The ISO (International Standards Organization) definition of an icon states that it must be able to be manipulated, such as moved or deleted. Traditionally, an icon has been paired with a label to reinforce both its function and its style or category. The icon's design can help to represent not only its content but its format. As an example, an icon can visually represent its file's particular format without the need to have a Label. Icons have also been required to display a file's current state, indicating whether the document or application was closed, opened, selected, or not available for selection. These different states would be indicated by varying the style of the icon image and traditionally have been represented as inversed or grayed bitmap images.

There is some danger of creating too many types of icons. We are beginning to realize that you can end up with too many icons on the screen that convey too many different meanings. When you create so many varying functions with only icons to represent their functions, the user begins to get confused as to which icon represents which function. The user is forced to start remembering too many different types of icon images and their functions. This situation would not be much of an improvement from many programs' current interface, which requires users to remember the many varieties of keystrokes. Adding to the confusion can be the fact that operations on icons vary. Some icons may be able to invoke a command, and others may be used to maximize a minimized application. Some icons must be double-clicked in true traditional icon form, and others require only a single mouse click. Some icons can be dragged, as can the ones used in a file manager application, and others cannot. Careful thought and restraint in the use of icons should be exercised by the application developer. Icons should not be created just for the sake of adding visual flair but should instead be developed when they will help to explain a function or a classification to the user.

In the world of Motif, there are two types of icons. The first type, Minimized Windows, consists of graphical images that represent an application that has been minimized but that is still running. Such windows require a window frame around them and are displayed either on the screen or in an Icon Box. The second type, Pictograms, consists of symbols placed instead of a Label on the background of a panel or a widget. A third type that we have designed into our product HP VUE (Visual User Environment) 2.0 is the manipulable file icon. These icons represent files or applications that are closed and not running. Manipulable file icons reside in a file manager window and can be moved, duplicated, or deleted. Figure 6–1 shows the three types of icons we use in HP VUE 2.0, based on Motif.

FIGURE 6–1 The three types of icons used in HP VUE are minimized windows, manipulable icons, and pictograms. Manipulable icons are not standard Motif icons.

Minimized Windows

Manipulable Icons

Pictograms

Icon Design

When you are designing icons for use with your particular application, a clear strategy for which types of icons are required will be of great help. Will the icons be used simply for symbolic labeling in a widget, or will they be required to indicate different states? Will they be substitutes for the label, or will they have to emphasize the function and be combined visually with the label? Will they represent files or executables that can be moved about in a file window, or will they represent graphical choices in an application? These subtle differences can enhance your application or create chaos.

Icons can be symbolic, whimsical, literal, or abstract. The user should be able to quickly identify and associate the icon image with the appropriate tool or document. In designing icons, you should keep the icon a familiar symbol in the user's established field of interest or expertise. In any profession or field of interest there are a number of symbolic representations that convey functional expectations that have been well established throughout the field's history. Research in the professional area for which you are designing as far as symbolic recognition will help a great deal before you start to design a set of icons. For example, icons for an application that is used in the medical field should clearly connote their individual functions while keeping the style and character of the icon within the visual expectations of the medical field. The same would hold true of other professional fields or fields of interest for which you would be designing.

Icons that have to represent abstract concepts, however, require a bit more imagination. There is usually no reference set of symbols from which to choose. The icon must therefore express either the application's function or simply the application's name. In the computing field there are a number of applications whose function cannot be described using a symbol that connotes its function. We must at times rely on the whimsical image or simply use a play on words. As an example, we designed our HP Softbench debugger tool icon to represent a squashed bug as a play on words while being whimsical. In situations such as these, the notion of a metaphor becomes very useful. Icon images or symbols can be metaphorical representations of the application's function. When designing a family of icons that must relate to a common theme, it is a good idea to design a common visual cue that is identifiable in each icon. Each icon in the set of icons that we designed for the "Softbench" suite of software development applications carries a common theme as well as the product name "SoftBench." Figure B–4 (color section) shows an example of a family of icons representing applications that are abstract functions.

Two-Dimensional or Three-Dimensional Icons?

There are two techniques in the design of our icons; two-dimensional and three-dimensional. These visual techniques are used with the limitation of having only two colors available for any bitmapped image — the bitmap foreground and background colors. When should an icon be two-dimensional and when should it be three-dimensional? There are possibilities for both types in your application.

Three-dimensional icons would be best represented with a minimum of three colors. A combination of top shadow, background, and bottom shadow colors would provide the optimum minimum set of the three colors that are required to create visually convincing three-dimensional icons. Because the X window system supports only two colors in any bit-mapped image, we are forced to use dithering techniques to achieve any three-dimensional visual effect. Three-dimensional icons are becoming increasingly popular because of their rich visual quality. Even when they are restricted to a dithered style with only two colors to play with, they represent a visually exciting alternative to the relatively flat images that we have become accustomed to over the years. This three-dimensional visual effect has been used as minimized window icons as well as in pictogram icons in Motif's message dialog boxes. Figure 6–2 shows the three-dimensional effect used as the Message dialog box icons.

This dithered three-dimensional effect is useful wherever there is enough space to render it in a convincing style. This effect is not recommended for use in tight areas. There is another tradeoff with using this technique. The dithered effect, although visually rich, can be less effective if your icon is required to show varying states in an obvious manner. This is because the image's background color is produced by using a 50-percent dithered pattern as the mid-range background color. When the usual method of inverting the two colors in the icon is used, the 50-percent dither may show little or no difference. Also, any inverted image using this technique will look as if the light source has shifted to the opposite direction, forcing the image to look like a film negative. When you are designing a three-dimensional icon that requires quick visual differences, design the icon so that the image shows enough of either the foreground or the background color so that an inverted image is visually obvious. Figure 6–3 shows a dithered icon with enough of the foreground color shown as a solid area that an inverted state is obvious.

Two-dimensional icons are bitmapped images that do not have any visual three-dimensional quality. They are flat in appearance with no hint of the image protruding in or out from the background surface. This technique has been used throughout the industry in most of the past and

Information

Query

Warning

Cannot Perform

Work In Progress

FIGURE 6–2 The three-dimensional effect shown in Message dialog box icons. These icons were designed using only two colors using a technique called *dithering*.

3-D icon

Inversed 3-D icon

FIGURE 6–3 Dithered techniques can hide the fact that the icon colors are inverted. This icon shows enough foreground color that it is obvious that it has been inverted.

present GUIs. Because of the nature of this visual technique, such icons can be designed as smaller images than three-dimensional icons. Two-dimensional icons would be represented fairly well with a minimum of two colors, because foreground and background colors are all that are needed to create these types of images. We have reserved the use of two-dimensional icons for tight areas where there is not enough space to render a three-dimensional image. Two-dimensional icons are also preferred as pictograms that are to be used instead of text, such as in a Label or on a Pushbutton where space is very limited. Two-dimensional icons should also be considered in situations in which you might have a large number of icons. Depending on the result, the two-dimensional style in this situation might help reduce the visual clutter often caused by Labels.

The use of two-dimensional icons is also recommended as an alternative to Labels in Pushbuttons, in which the select color must be shown to convey selection. The two-dimensional icon should retain its foreground color while the background of the Pushbutton changes to the slightly darker select color upon selection. Figure 6–4 shows the icons used in widgets and in tight places.

FIGURE 6–4 Pictogram icons should be used in widgets that benefit from an icon but that are situated in tight places. Icons can sometimes convey information that would otherwise necessitate a large amount of space for Labels.

Pictogram Design

Pictograms are the simplest of the three types of icons mentioned in this chapter. They are icons that are used as symbols or labels of a function. They are not required to be moved or deleted, nor are they required to show state changes. They are typically designed in two-dimensional fashion and are often used as alternatives to Labels. There are times when the three-dimensional visual quality used in a minimized window icon may be desirable in widgets such as Pushbuttons. Earlier in this chapter, an example of three-dimensional pictograms was shown in which the icons served as the symbols for the Message dialog boxes. This three-dimensional technique should be used only when the widget's function is more clearly expressed by these rich icons than by Labels or two-dimensional icons. The following two examples will illustrate how we have used this technique in application areas.

This dithering pattern was incorporated for the design of the pictogram icons used in the "Dashboard" workspace utility front panel in HP VUE 2.0. The design called for a unique dashboard-type panel that would house the most often used functions in your screen workspace. Pictograms were used to display icons that would communicate each function without the need for text labels in each Pushbutton. Because these Pushbuttons are not susceptible to changes in size from text translation, their pictograms were able to be designed to extend to the edges of each Pushbutton. The result is a set of integrated Pushbuttons that appear sculpted with their icons. Figure B–1 (color section) shows the "Dashboard" displaying its pictogram Pushbuttons.

In the "Style Manager" customizing application for HP VUE 2.0, pictograms were designed for use as the symbols for the Pushbuttons that invoke the array of various customizing functions. Unlike those in the Dashboard, these pictograms had to be designed in a way that would allow each Pushbutton to incorporate its Label underneath. Translation of these Labels sometimes forced the Labels to be wider than the pictograms. Because pictograms cannot change their size with the size of the Pushbuttons, each pictogram was designed so that it would appear appropriate when centered side to side in each Pushbutton. Each pictogram's top and bottom shadow was incorporated into its visual design using the dithered technique. The result was a set of pictograms that appeared appropriate for any width Pushbutton. Figure B–8 (color section) shows an example of pictogram icons used in Pushbuttons for the Style Manager.

This three-dimensional technique can add a richer appearance to your application interface. As with minimized window icons, any two colors can be used for these icon images. I recommend using the top and bottom shadow colors of the Pushbutton's background color. This will provide enough contrast to display the icon image. Use these two colors in a 50-percent dither to give the illusion that the icon is drawn with the same color as the Pushbutton's background color. If the widget's top and bottom shadow colors are not appropriate, a neutral set of colors that is visually compatible with the widget's background color is recommended. When using the three-dimensional technique for pictograms in a Pushbutton, make sure that the Pushbutton is not required to fill its center with the select color upon selection. If this is required, the three-dimensional pictogram will look awkward when its surrounding is filled with the select color. Because contrasting colors tend to bloom when displayed in high resolution, the human eye will average the different values of the top and bottom shadow colors as one color when displayed in a 50-percent dithered pattern. Any pictogram bitmap is constrained to be designed within a rectangle. Figure 6–5 shows the various visual components to consider when designing a pictogram.

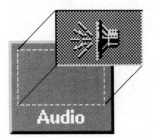 

FIGURE 6–5 Pictograms are bitmaps that can be placed on a button to emphasize functionality.

Icon Design for Manipulable Files

Manipulable file icons were designed for use in our proprietary user environment for direct manipulation of iconified files and applications. This type of icon represents a closed document or directory and is able to be moved, copied, or deleted. These icons are designed to be displayed only in a window that has file management capabilities. Selection states must also be shown in these icon types. Figure B–5 (color section) shows how these types of icons are used in HP's "File Manager" file manipulation application.

These icons can be designed using both the two-dimensional and three-dimensional techniques. The directory icons were designed with the dithered technique to convey a three-dimensional effect, and the document icon was designed as a flat two-dimensional image. The two techniques served to express the different nature of these two types of files. The three-dimensional technique was used in the directory icon to convey the idea that other files and documents can be placed within it. The two-dimensional technique, on the other hand, was used for individual documents to convey that nothing can go inside of them. Figure 6–6 shows an example of manipulable icons in a file manager window.

32 x 32 pixel icons

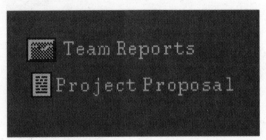

16 x 16 pixel icons

FIGURE 6–6 These manipulable icons designed for the File Manager in HP's VUE were designed in two sizes so that a user can select between displaying large icons (approximately 32-by-32 pixels) and small icons (approximately 16-by-16 pixels).

Icon Design for Minimized Windows

Minimized windows are application windows that are still running and that are minimized into icons for the sake of reducing the number of windows on the screen. These are represented as application icons with window frames around them. The icon for these windows should represent the appropriate application's function. The dithered effect should be used here to create a three-dimensional visual quality to the icon. Application icons can be designed in any two colors. If the application that the icon represents is designed with two color sets, with the Menubar being a different color from the application's work area, I recommend using the top and bottom shadow colors of the Menubar as the foreground and background colors of the icon. Using its parent application's Menubar colors will help the user distinguish this icon from other applications' icons. This color coding will also help to reassure the user visually that the application that was minimized is represented as an icon. Figure 6–7 shows the icons used to represent minimized windows.

The colors in minimized application icons can be specified in the resources **Mwm*iconImageForeground** and **Mwm*iconImageBackground**. These resources should be set to the application's Menubar top and bottom shadow colors. The use of these two extreme colors will be interpreted by the human eye as the average of the two and will give the illusion that the minimized window icon image is the same color as the application's Menubar when drawn with the dithered technique. Use the following resources to set the correct colors of the icon image:

> **Mwm*iconImageTopShadowColor**
> **Mwm*iconImageBottomShadowColor**
> **Mwm*iconImageTopShadowPixmap**
> **Mwm*iconImageBottomShadowPixmap**

The top shadow color should be specified as the foreground color used in the icon image, and the bottom shadow color should be specified as the background color in the icon image. Design the background of the icon image in a 50-percent dithered pattern to each edge. Doing this enables the top and bottom shadow colors to appear against the dithered icon background color. Any icon that is designed as a minimized window icon is constrained by default to be a 50-by-50 pixel bitmap.

Motif's Window Manager requires a window frame around any minimized window icon. The window frame surrounding the icon provides a title below the icon image. When the icon has the input focus, its

FIGURE 6–7 A minimized window icon's visual components.

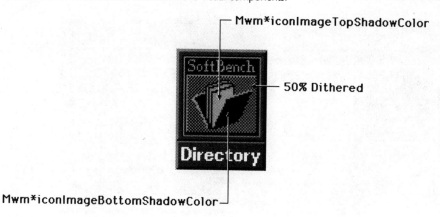

window frame changes to the bright active color. The title is normally truncated to the width of the icon. When the icon is selected with the mouse, the title expands to show the title name in its entirety. Figure 6–8 shows Motif's Icon frame.

Icons can be displayed either on the screen background or, if specified, in an Icon Box. Motif provides this optional Icon Box as a way to keep icons of minimized windows organized in one place. The Icon Box behaves much like a standard application window with resizable borders and scrollbars. The icons are displayed within the Scrolled Window and can be scrolled to and selected. The icon box also allows the applications to be moved to the top of a stack of other application windows by clicking on the icon image associated with its window. Figure 6–9 shows Motif's Icon Box.

FIGURE 6–8 A minimized icon frame.

FIGURE 6–9 Motif's optional Icon Box.

Motif's Visual Design Principles

Design Principles

7

Chapter

The fact that you are even looking at this book proves that you have an interest in using Motif as the Graphical User Interface for your application designs. The fact that you are thinking about using Motif proves that you are one of the growing number of application designers who are concerned about how easy your computer applications are to use for people other than programmers. In the past, applications and functions in the computer required the user to understand a variety of keystrokes and play the endless guessing game of what to type in next just to invoke a function. These functions could be done with a command line or with a combination of keystrokes. This was fine for people who had the time to learn these skills. It wasn't fine for the majority of the people who wanted to or were required to use computers. This would be like having to learn the wiring schematics of an ignition system for each different car you drive in order to start each car. People who didn't or couldn't learn this would be out of luck and wouldn't be able to drive. Fortunately, this isn't how cars turned out, and with all the different GUIs on the market, it looks as though the computer will eventually evolve in the same direction. Unfortunately, we are not there yet. Instead, we are in the midst of the change that will someday be recognized as the event that brought us to the standard usable computer for the masses.

With this in mind, you should start thinking about how an end user is going to use your software package. At every stage of the design of your application, the question of "How" from an end user's point of view will be the most important question that you can ask yourself. How will the user call up a file? How will the user delete that file? How will the user edit the file? How will the user create something new in the file? You get the point. In designing your application, you can assume that not all of the users of your application will be computer scientists, nor will they have the time and inclination to learn how to become such experts. In fact, it would be in your best interest not to want your audience to be only software engineers, as that narrows your market tremendously. The mass market or domain-specific markets are much larger and should be your target audience for any application. The days of writing applications only for people who understand the ins and outs of programming are fast disappearing.

General Design Guidelines

There is a growing need for domain-specific computing applications. This includes all walks of people, professionals, interests, and hobbies. There are needs for prewritten applications that are simple to use and understand, as well as tools that will help a nonprogramming person have access to the power of the computer for his/her own specific needs. These people are successful in their fields of endeavor and simply want access to the benefits of the computer. Typically, they do not have the time or the inclination to learn details about computers. If a doctor or an engineer spent most of the time learning how to program or learning the programming languages associated with a particular application, there wouldn't be much time left over to actually practice medicine or engineering. We all have needs for a variety of machines in our lives, from toasters to televisions, from cars to can openers. These devices add convenience and empower us to pursue activities of higher personal interest. We are discovering that computers can help us try new ideas or shorten a tedious task. They can help control boring, repetitive tasks and help us explore and visualize concepts that we previously could only dream about.

Designing an application, like designing anything, requires time up front for researching the intended market's needs and expectations. Before even thinking about your first line of code for an application, you should spend some time understanding who will use this application and how they will expect to use it.

Taking a few steps to question and evaluate your new concept will help you establish a direction and set a design goal for your application. It is important to establish a design goal early in the project so that you can keep focused on who the end user of your application will be. This will also influence how you intend to go about designing it. As an application designer, no matter what your professional background, whether it be programming, engineering, science, or business, you probably already know more technically about what you want to offer than those for whom you are writing this application for. You have identified a need that isn't currently filled in the marketplace. You already have in mind a solution to this need in terms of a new software application. The task that you face is to design an application that will present this capability to users in a way they can understand and that will convince them that it will help them do their tasks in a better way. Welcome to the design process!

Earlier I mentioned that you need to establish a design goal. This is very important because it is what will keep you focused on the design issues of your application. A design goal can be simply that the application will be easy to use and as aesthetically pleasing as possible. This is a good start, but your goal can be more detailed. A design goal is a set of standards that you should set out to achieve in the design of your application. Design goals can include tailoring your application specifically to your intended market, or designing it so that it will have broad aesthetic appeal. Another design goal might be to excite the user in a positive way. A task might be complex, warranting a reward for users at the end of a job well done. This would be a design goal as well. Anything that can enhance the user's experience without disrupting the task should be considered in your design goal list. Your application should be designed so that it not only performs satisfactorily but also enhances the user's enjoyment of using your application. Special attention should be paid to the user's needs and expectations.

These next steps will help you think about your application and its design direction. Aside from the obvious technical concerns of your application, the following set of nontechnical questions and attitudes will help set design goals for your application's design.

Who Is the
Audience?

Will they be professional people? What do they do? Are they doctors, lawyers, engineers, artists, accountants? Should your application design communicate to a combination of a few of these professions?

It is important to know who your audience is. They will use your application with a whole set of preconceived notions and expectations of what your application could do for them. Most professions have deep-rooted traditions and symbolic images. In designing icons, a triangle and a brush can have clear meaning for artists but probably mean nothing to a doctor. A grid can evoke notions of a spreadsheet to an accountant, whereas it can mean something entirely different to an engineer. Selecting the right words for use as labels in your application's interface can sometimes be confusing depending on your audience. Every profession has its own jargon, which has meaning only to that circle of professionals. Be cautious in using jargon. The words used in your application should be simple and understandable by the majority of people. These preconceived notions are important to understand if your application is to be successful in communicating with your audience. Design your application to be logical, intuitive, and responsive to people's general expectations. In this way, you will be successful in communicating the application's functions.

What Is the Level
of Expectation of
the End User?

What does your audience expect? When people use anything, they already have preconceived notions of what to expect both behaviorally and visually. The question of expectation can be to the benefit or detriment of your design. Expectations are formed from experience. In the world of Motif, users will learn to expect certain behaviors and visual changes after invoking certain functions. This expectation will be learned from other applications built from Motif. Expectations will also be learned from your application for use in other applications. If you have designed a new function or a way to manipulate a new device, it should be designed with the intention of adding to instead of replacing the existing behavioral and visual language that is characteristic to Motif. For instance, if you found a way to add functionality to an existing Pushbutton and the result would be a specially functioning Pushbutton with a modified appearance for special purposes in your applications, this would probably be acceptable and will be learned by your audience. If, however, you decide that the current Pushbutton should invoke a command fundamentally different from a standard Pushbutton, this would surprise users abruptly with an unexpected behavior and would be unacceptable.

Do not use anything that will surprise users while they are concentrating on a task. With some programs on the market right now, users can be doing intricate work and the software will do something startling, breaking the users' train of thought. For example, with one CAD (Computer

Aided Design) program on the market, every time users place a modeled object in a new position, the screen blinks white for a split second and blinds the users while the computer is refreshing the screen with the new image. This unexpected behavior is very disruptive to users. Often in this situation, users forget what they were thinking about. Users trust your application to operate consistently with other applications, and they tend to expect the best, not the worst.

Is Your Application Intuitive to Use?

Your application should be as intuitive as possible for the end user. Most users of your application will become proficient over time, but you should still design it for both novice and experienced users. Experienced users are still novices to new functionality that they haven't tried yet. *Intuitive* doesn't mean that your application should be designed so that it sacrifices performance for ease of use. When I say *intuitive,* I mean that all of the functionality of your application should behave in a manner that makes the best cognitive sense to the end user. The functions of an application should make sense the first time a user uses it and should be designed as a fundamental part of the application's functionality. In the automobile, the steering wheel is intuitive in its functionality. As you turn the wheel to the left, the car is directed to the left. As novice drivers become more experienced, they do not give up the steering wheel in favor of a faster, more abstract way of steering the car. In other words, design your application's functionality in a way that makes the most sense to people's natural behavior.

How Will Your Users Invoke the Task?

As mentioned earlier, the question of "How" will be the test in evaluating the design of your application. When designing your application for use in a graphical user environment, you must continually ask yourself "How is the user going to perform this task?" You cannot assume that the user has even an inkling of the correct function keystrokes or your application will fail. If you require the user to change a setting in order to invoke a function, you must provide the provisions for the user to change that setting effortlessly. If you conclude that this can be changed in the X defaults, or the resource file, your application will have failed. These instances are the weakest links in your application. Attention must be given to the most minute detail in order to provide the end user with a seamless way to interact with the computer through intuitive means of direct manipulation. Once you determine in your development that the user could go to the terminal window and type in the appropriate commands to specify a function, your application is no longer useful to 90 percent of your potential users. The only people who can and might deal with this would be people with programming knowledge, but I wouldn't count on it.

When your end users, who are most likely domain professionals and not programmers, encounter this situation and all of a sudden are expected to access a terminal window and type in "X" commands, they will be stumped. To end users, this is the equivalent of the computer saying, "For your next task you have to guess what to type in and I am not going to give you any hints." Most users won't even have a clue. Many applications turn out to be incredible guessing games. This is why it is important to ask continually, "How is the user going to do that?" It is also a good idea to design in dialog prompts to lead the user to an intelligent choice when it is not obvious what to do next.

Always Present the User with a Choice

When designing an application with multiple capabilities that require the user to set parameters, show the user all of the appropriate choices. Do not expect him/her to remember the choices from a manual or a reference card. Chances are that the reference card will get lost and someone else will have borrowed the manual. You should not require users to type in their choices, either. Design your application so that choices are clearly displayed, whether in the main application, in the Menubar, or in a dialog box. Let the user simply select from the best alternatives in a given situation. Minimize the amount of typing required to make the same choices over and over again. Let the user choose. Your user has more important things to think about than remembering how to type a command correctly.

Stick with Domain-Specific Metaphors

Metaphors are useful concepts for visualizing the character of your application. When trying to describe a concept or an idea to friends who haven't quite grasped the level of understanding you have, you might try to describe it with a metaphor to illustrate it in a way that helps them to relate to it better. The metaphor of an automobile has been used many times to describe the goal of commonality and intuitive behavior of human-computer interfaces, because most people can relate to its functions. This helps to illustrate to the rest of us why these efforts are so important. The same applies at the level of the individual application. When designing an application, you should assume that it will be partially or completely new to the public. Because people draw on experiences to understand a concept, basing your application design on a metaphor that can be easily identified by your audience can be beneficial to the success of the application design. Different domains will have different metaphors. A metaphor used in a manufacturing environment will be different from a metaphor in the teaching environment.

Design Your Application with Progressive Disclosure in Mind

Your application should be designed so that the user can exercise progressive disclosure. Progressive disclosure is very important in a graphically designed user interface, because it allows the user to explore through the application without getting into trouble. The user should be able to search through menu choices and invoke dialog boxes that will give messages or provide fill-in areas that will give the user a sense of the application's functions. The disclosure of capabilities and functions can do wonders to help new users quickly assess the usefulness of your application to their needs. Users should be able to go at their own pace and not be committed to invoke any functions that may be intimidating. Any erroneous selections that may erase or change the application should be combined with a warning so that users have a chance to back out of any mistaken choice of function.

Storyboard Your Concepts

Storyboarding is a technique that has been used by the movie industry to help people visualize quickly and inexpensively the character and flow of a movie before any time or money is spent in producing it. This technique has been very useful in conveying an application design to potential users. Storyboarding techniques can also be very helpful in the design of applications. Because an application with a graphical user interface is visual information constantly in motion, this technique has proven to be very useful. The clearer this visual information or dialog is, the clearer the functionality of the application will be to the potential user. The use of up-front storyboarding in the design of an application can uncover many questions regarding the potential user's understanding of the capabilities of your application. It can also uncover opportunities for incorporating new and improved visual methods for communicating information such as transition effects and timing of certain functions.

Storyboards can vary in technique from a simple set of hand-drawn illustrations to full-blown animations. Storyboarding will help cut expensive prototyping time and will reveal any unclear user models or concepts even before any code has been written. Storyboards can start out as hand-drawn sketches and, as time and budget warrants, can be made into interactive demos that can reveal your potential user's understanding and expectations of the capabilities of your application.

Design Methodologies

The design process can lead you through several stages before any coding will even take place. As in designing anything, the more concepts you evaluate up front, the more questions will be answered. There will also be opportunities where discoveries and new ideas will be uncovered. The design process will add some time up front to your application design but the effort will be well worth it. It is much better to conceptualize and then evaluate than to go in the wrong direction and find out when it is too late. The following stages will help structure the design process of your application.

The Concept Stage

This is the conceptual stage in which all new ideas should be played out. Your new application may warrant a new way of performing or displaying a function. This is where new ideas can be expressed quickly and effortlessly. New ideas are always in the minds of people creating new applications. You should look at these ideas here before you commit to more irreversible techniques. This is the stage at which the overall concept should be sketched out in an inexpensive and time-efficient medium, such as sketching with pencil and paper. With colleagues, you can use group brainstorm situations with a white board and easily erasable markers to explore new ideas. The more time spent in this area, the less time will be wasted later in developing concepts that are inappropriate to the design goals of your application. If you use these techniques and free yourself of the constraints of the computer, ideas will flow quickly and effortlessly. These ideas can be shared with others in the team to get immediate feedback on their opinions and concerns of the direction in which you are headed.

Design Stage

Concepts that are the most promising from the concept stage should be illustrated using a paint program or some prototyping builder application. I tend to favor a computer-based paint program because it allows me the freedom to explore new ideas with visually accurate results. By illustrating these concepts in a visually accurate form, you will be able to examine all of the visual details associated with your design. Answers to many visual design questions will begin to emerge. Details such as widget layout and alignment, as well as proportion and size of your application, will be revealed by illustrating the concept at this level of detail. Analysis of the ergonomic quality of your application can be assessed as well. Are scrollbars wide enough? Is the font legible? Is there enough contrast between the foreground and background colors? These are just a few of the questions whose answers will reveal themselves. A paint program that will display designs in the correct display resolution will help immensely in visualizing accurately what your final design will look like. It will also help clear up any questions others have about your approach to your application design.

Animation Stage

A picture is worth a thousand words, and in the industrial design profession, a model is worth a thousand pictures. In Visual User Interface Design, we are quickly realizing that an animation is worth a thousand models. Nothing in my experience explains a concept more clearly than an animation. All the verbal explanation and hand-waving with drawings cannot equal the presentation power of a simple animation to illustrate your concept. This is the stage at which the most appropriate concept is set into motion so that all of its most subtle detail can be experienced visually instead of verbally. With animation, there is nothing to interpret. The behavior and resultant visual design of your application is represented in the animation. It mimics how the application will behave.

This is also the opportunity for exploring transition effects in the user interface realm. With Motif as a foundation for the basic user interface components, much of the solutions will encompass transition effects. These effects, which can be visual as well as auditory, can greatly enhance the user's total working experience with the computer. Transition effects can be helpful in assuring the user that a task is being accomplished. These effects can also serve to help warn the user of problems, such as limited memory space or that the system is about to shut down. Visual design effects of this type cannot be illustrated adequately with still images. Writing code to demonstrate these effects is also not cost-effective.

A computer-based animation program works the best for this, preferably one that will take your computer-based paint images and put them in motion in a compelling and realistic manner.

Animation can be used to evaluate a number of functions. It can be used to evaluate transition effects, such as how an icon might turn into an application window, as well as what a color change can do to a screen of applications. Animations can reveal a user's expectations of performance by speeding up or slowing down a function.

In addition to analyzing transition effects, animations can be used to approximate the timing of changes to see how the user's expectations are met in terms of the timing or location of events. Some animation applications are now offering varying degrees of interactivity. This can be used to test various aspects of the user's dialog with the application by actually involving potential users.

Prototype or Coding Stage

This is the stage in which, after your concept has been approved, the coding of the real thing takes place. It is useful at this stage to use a builder or a prototyping program for acting out your application design. A builder is helpful in determining the interaction of your application, both with the user and with the functions that it must perform. A builder can also be used by the application designer to test that the widgets are signaling the correct functions. A prototyping builder is also of great benefit for testing widget relationships. It will let you do anything as long as it conforms to its established set of widgets.

Motif provides a variety of functionality that forms a visual and behavioral foundation for the design of most applications. All of this functionality, with its three-dimensional widgets does not, however, guarantee ergonomically correct or visually pleasing applications. Nor does it guarantee that the application will contain the correct metaphor for the market audience for which you are designing. That must come from you, the application designer. It is up to your imagination to make use of these interface components. If you do not have the methodologies that will enable you to research the characteristics of your intended audience, seek it out in the form of a professional who does. If it is visual design help you are looking for, seek it out in an experienced user interface designer. If it is ergonomic help you are looking for, seek it out in an experienced human factors engineer. The world of graphically designed applications is becoming more and more competitive from the point of view of ease of use and visual design, and the more help you can get, the better.

Application Design Guidelines

8

Chapter

In this chapter, I will discuss design layout principles that will help you create aesthetically and ergonomically pleasing application windows. In addition, I will describe the fundamental design layout configurations using Motif's widgets. These guidelines can help you organize the visual layout of your application's interface using Motif widgets. The end result should be an application that is visually pleasing and easy to understand. These guidelines are provided to enable you to design applications that allow sufficient work area in your application for the user to do the required task while maintaining a level of consistency and visual quality that makes for an aesthetically appealing application.

The process of laying out widgets for your application can benefit greatly if you spend some time thinking about the spacing details that can make the difference between an attractive, functional application window and an application window that just contains widgets. Attention to detail, such as consistent spacing between widgets as well as visual organization of functional areas, will help provide an aesthetically pleasing interface.

General Guideline Rules

Before laying out widgets in your application window, you need to pay attention to two areas. The traversal highlight thickness and the size and style of fonts should be determined beforehand. These two areas will greatly affect the appearance of your application.

The traversal highlight thickness should be predetermined and set for every widget that you use. By default, this thickness is set to 2 pixels, and you can use this setting. Because all widgets are spaced from the edge of the traversal highlight, this will ensure consistent positioning of your widgets when they are laid out onto the application window. At a later time, whether or not you decide to set the traversal highlight to appear will not affect the relative positioning of your widgets. There will be times when the thickness of the traversal highlight will be used as the appropriate spacing between widgets. Figure 8–1 shows how widgets are lined up and how the traversal highlight thickness affects their alignment.

FIGURE 8–I Traversal highlight thickness can be used as the required spacing between widgets, which eliminates the need to specify a distance between widgets. This example shows that a traversal thickness of 2 pixels will make Pushbuttons appear to be spaced 4 pixels apart.

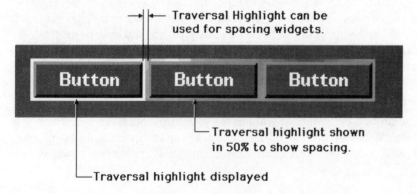

Traversal highlight thickness set to 2 pixels for this example.

Fonts should be consistent throughout your application, as mentioned in chapter 3. If they are not of the same height or style, your widgets will suffer visually because Motif's widget sizing is determined by the font size within each widget. For instance, if you use one font size in a Push-button and another size in a Text widget and attempt to line them up in the same row, the one with the larger font will be displayed with its bottom edge lower than the other widget. Motif's widgets are lined up by their managers from the top and left edges. This means that if a widget has a font that is even one pixel different in height from the others, the visual effect will be such that it won't line up by one pixel. Figure 8–2 shows how varying the font size within an application can affect the size and alignment of widgets.

Widget Layout Guidelines

When the time comes to decide on the visual placement of widgets in an application window, it is important to determine their layout in such a way that the result will be visually consistent and logical to the user. In this example, let's use a conceptual application to discuss widget layout guidelines. I designed a conceptual application called Mail for this example to better illustrate how different widgets should be laid out in an application window. Currently, most existing applications employ only a few widgets and are not well suited for this example.

FIGURE 8–2 Varying the font size within an application affects the size of widgets and causes misalignment of similar widgets.

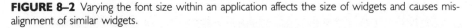

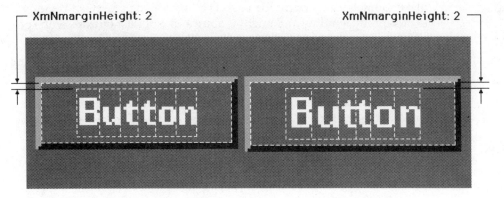

After going through the conceptual and storyboarding stages, as mentioned in chapter 7, you are ready to start placing widgets in their proper places in an application. The first thing to do is to determine the basic layout of the major manager widgets, such as the Menubar or special tool or function areas such as text entry, text display, and function areas such as Pushbuttons. The layout of these functional areas should have been predetermined from the design process phase of developing this application.

Basic Motif-compliant layout principles include placing the Menubar at the top of the client area. If there are special cases in which the Menubar will be best placed somewhere other than at the top, it is up to you to determine that. But for the most part, placing the Menubar at the top of the application window puts it where most users would expect to find it, as well as complying with the OSF/Motif Style Guide. Figure 8–3 shows the Menubar placement in the Mail application window.

After you place the Menubar at the top of the window's client area, the example application requires a Paned Window in order for it to be split into two functional areas. The Paned Window is very useful for applications that require two or more distinct functional areas. This provides two adjustable work areas without requiring the window to be resized, in addition to allowing it to be space efficient and prevent it from dominating the screen. Figure 8–4 shows Paned Windows configured for the application.

In this application, each Pane in the Paned Window is surrounded by a 1-pixel Frame widget. This provides a visual quality to the Panes and gives them an appearance of being separated from the Window Frame. Figure 8–5 shows the Frame widget surrounding the Paned Window.

After you have configured the Paned Window, each Pane contains a Scrolled Window. Scrolled Windows in an application should be configured to span the width of the application window. This will provide the maximum reading area for the user. The upper Pane's Scrolled Window is a read only window and might require a row of Pushbuttons with specific functions assigned to that window. These could be functions like Print, Forward, Read Next, and Delete. From your analysis, you have determined that the proper place for these Pushbuttons is directly below the Scrolled Window. The proper configuration for Pushbuttons in an application window is to specify them so that they are forced to line up in a row while not forcing their width to any one size. Figure 8–6 shows the upper Scrolled Window with Pushbuttons placed in the work area.

FIGURE 8–3 The Menubar is placed in the Mailer application window at the top of the client area. This complies with OSF/Motif's style guide.

FIGURE 8–4 Paned Windows are configured for the Mailer application.

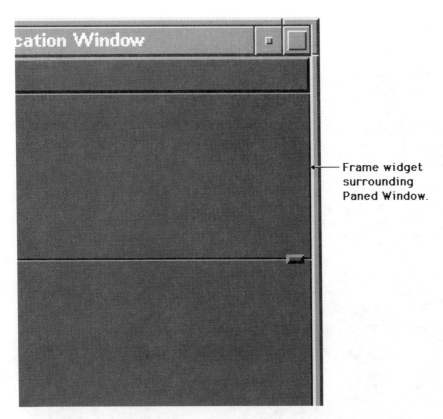

Frame widget
surrounding
Paned Window.

FIGURE 8–5 A 1-pixel Frame widget is used to surround the Paned Windows. This gives a refined appearance to the edges of the panes.

Consistency in spacing is the key to the appearance of this example. Each widget, whether a Label, a Scrolled Window, or a Pushbutton, is spaced consistently from one another. A pixel dimension of 4 was used in this example. Because we used the default traversal highlight thickness of 2, the required spacing was sometimes achieved by placing widgets right next to one another. The unhighlighted space of the traversal highlight provided the required spacing. Figures 8–7 and 8–8 show the consistency employed in the spacing of widgets in an application window.

The lower Pane contains a Scrolled Window that would be the window for writing a letter. This might also require a row of Pushbuttons with window-specific commands assigned to them. Again, the spacing of the

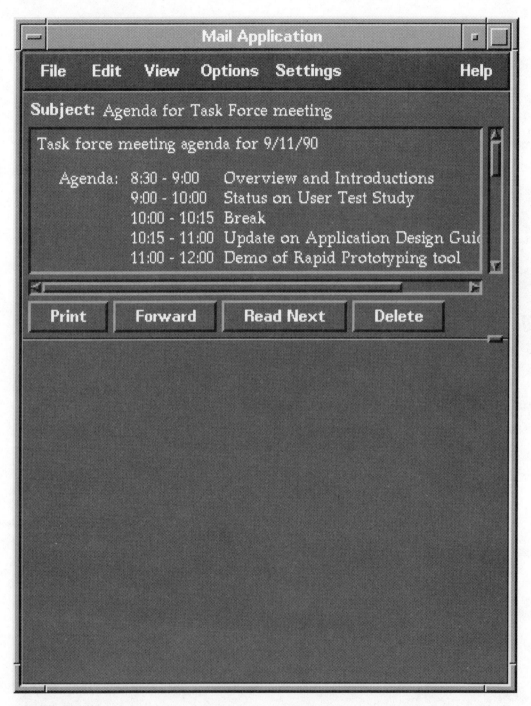

FIGURE 8–6 The Scrolled window with its Pushbuttons underneath is placed in the top Paned Window.

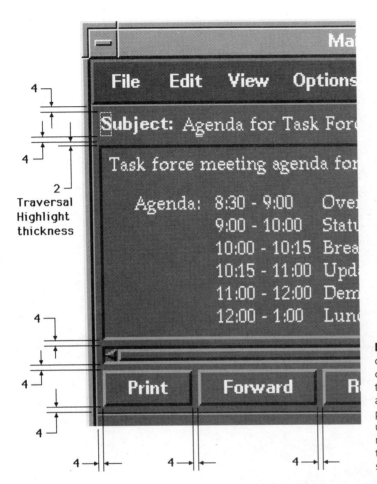

FIGURE 8–7 A close-up view of the left side of the Mailer application. This shows the consistency of spacing between widgets and provides for an attractive appearance. A spacing of 4 pixels is used between all widgets. In most cases, the traversal highlight thickness will provide the necessary spacing between widgets.

widgets is consistent and is similar in style to that in the upper Pane. All vertical spacing as well as horizontal spacing was kept at a consistent 4-pixel distance. Figure 8–9 shows the lower Paned Window filled with its widget layout.

Compare this example with the same application without close attention paid to its visual details. The following example shows what can happen when inconsistent spacing and font sizes are used. Figure 8–10 shows an overview of the same application without visual consistency.

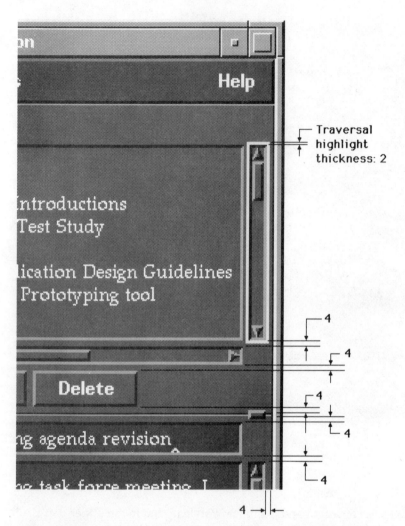

FIGURE 8–8 A close-up view of the right side of the Mailer application. Like figure 8–7, this shows the consistency of spacing between widgets and and the resultant attractive appearance.

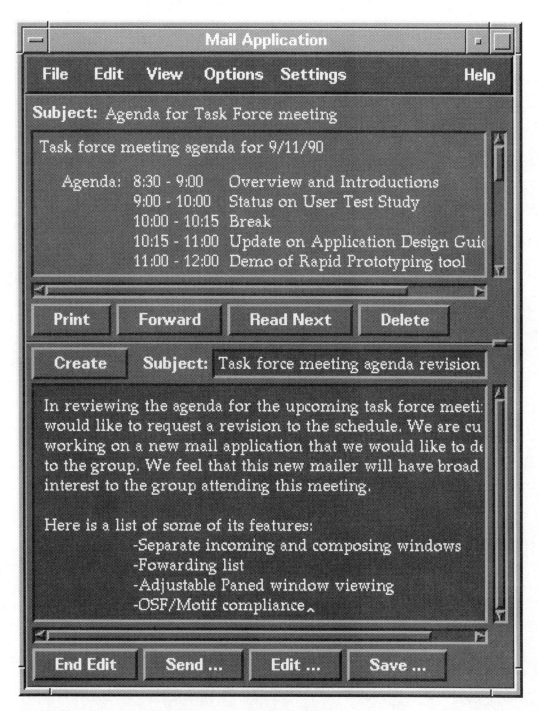

FIGURE 8–9 The lower Paned Window is shown filled with its widget layout.

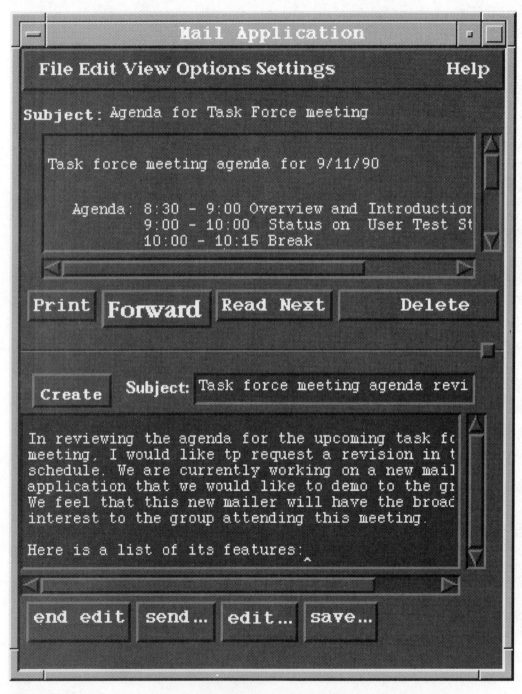

Compared with this example, the same application with a minimum of attention paid to the subtle visual details of widget layout might look disorganized and inconsistent. Careful attention to spacing consistency, and font size can help avoid disastrous results. Figure 8–11 shows a view of an application whose details were not tended to.

The following are some of the visual problems in the example shown in figure 8–11:

A. Menubar Labels are too close together, making it difficult to distinguish one topic from another. The font used is also rather large and appears clumsy.

B. Widgets are misaligned because of inconsistent margin heights.

C. The Scrolled Window's left edge is too far from the left edge of the Pane, creating a large area. This is wasted real screen estate.

D. The Window Frame is thick and can be configured to be thinner and visually more appealing.

E. A large margin was created by placing the Scrolled Window too far to the right.

F. Inconsistent font sizes in similar widgets cause misalignment of the Pushbuttons' Labels and an awkward appearance.

G. The space between the row of Pushbuttons and the Paned Window Separator is too generous. This wastes screen real estate and looks clumsy. This space should be configured to appear minimal for the best appearance.

H. Dissimilar widgets are misaligned because of lack of attention to make sure that margin heights between widgets are configured for consistent alignment.

I. Careless assignment of the top margin resulted in an overly large top margin area. This causes the label in a widget to be placed at the bottom portion of the widget.

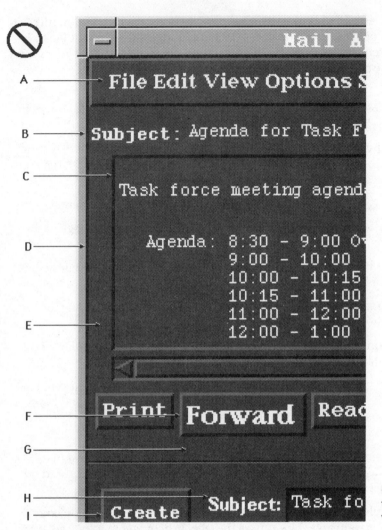

A —
B —
C —
D —
E —
F —
G —
H —
I —

File Edit View Options S

Subject: Agenda for Task F

Task force meeting agend

Agenda: 8:30 - 9:00 O
         9:00 - 10:00
         10:00 - 10:15
         10:15 - 11:00
         11:00 - 12:00
         12:00 - 1:00

Print   **Forward**   Read

Create   **Subject:** Task fo

Mail A

FIGURE 8–11 A close-up of the details that make this example visually unappealing.

Dialog Box Design Guidelines

9

Chapter

Dialog boxes serve an important and often misunderstood role in graphical user interfaces. The dialog box helps to display information or queries for information in much more detail than is visually possible in the application window. Many of the detailed functions that must be dealt with by a user do not occur frequently enough to warrant a dedicated space in the application window. They would be confusing if they were that persistent. Thanks to dialog boxes, most application developers can hide the mechanisms for getting detailed information and functions without cluttering the appearance of the main application window. Dialog boxes appear only when they are required.

Dialog Box Design Principles

Dialog box design guidelines are different from those of main application windows. Dialog boxes, unlike main application windows, can vary greatly depending on the information they must present to the user.

They must provide or ask for information that is both clear and concise without being overly large and cumbersome. Dialog box text and information should be brief and to the point. The user shouldn't have to read verbose text in order to understand what is being asked for or displayed by the dialog box. The flow of a dialog must be such that it can be read and comprehended at the speed at which the user is thinking. Dialog boxes should be laid out in such a manner that the user does not have to stop and break any train of thought before reacting to them.

Dialog boxes should also be context-specific. For instance, if a dialog box is spawned from selecting a print command, it should contain settings or queries regarding the printing of your document and nothing else.

As a convenience to application developers, OSF's Motif provides four predesigned dialog boxes. These are the ones that OSF thought would be used most often. They are Message, Selection, File Selection, and Command. However, as you design more specialized applications with greater capabilities, you will be faced with having to design sophisticated customized dialog boxes that will display clear and concise information.

Dialog Box Color Scheme

Applications designed using Motif are displayed in multiwindowed environments, and the varied applications that might be displayed can consume the screen quickly. Most applications will probably have dialog boxes associated with them. With modeless dialog boxes being the norm in most applications, the visual confusion will increase. As mentioned in chapter 2 on color, applications can be color-coded to help the user distinguish one application from another by color as well as title. Dialog boxes can be color-coded in a similar way. Because most dialog boxes should be designed to be spawned from the application's Menubar, they should take on the color of that Menubar. This would help the user to see which application spawned the dialog box. Figure A–7 (color section earlier in this book) shows dialog boxes color-coded to their application's Menubars.

Dialog Box Location

When a dialog box is spawned, it should appear in front of its application. Because a multiwindowed screen can fill up quickly with other application's dialog boxes, the new one can get lost in the multitude of dialog boxes already on the screen. A problem that I've noticed is that new dialog boxes frequently appear at the same location when spawned from the same application. The result is that subsequent dialog boxes appear one on top of the other. Because several dialog boxes may be used together at times, I recommend that each dialog box have a unique location assigned to it for display. A gradual stepping alignment scheme can be useful for displaying multiple dialog boxes from an application. Each dialog box can be located in a position that is slightly downward and to the right. Figure 9–1 shows dialog boxes positioned at a stepped interval from the previous one.

Design Guidelines for Laying Out Dialog Boxes

The same layout rules that apply in designing application windows also apply to dialog boxes with regard to colors, fonts, and traversal highlights. Consistency is the key here. Consistency also applies in widget dimensioning, resulting in predictable layouts of your widgets.

Unlike applications, dialog boxes do not have to adhere to prescribed visual design guidelines. There is room for design freedom, which will allow each dialog box to be designed in the layout that will best communicate its functionality. Dialog boxes can vary from simple queries, such as a confirmation that a file should be deleted, to more complex tasks, such as selecting a font from a wide variety of fonts. In designing the layout of a dialog box, keep in mind the following thoughts:

Think of dialog boxes as additional control panels. Dialog boxes are more than just notes with messages or labels on them. Their function is fundamental to the display and selection of detailed context-specific choices. You can specify that dialog boxes be modal or modeless. Modal dialog boxes require the user to respond to them before any further work can continue. Modeless dialog boxes do not require the user to respond to them and can be left on the screen and ignored as the user continues to work. In Motif, all dialog boxes with the exception of warnings are modeless and therefore can be treated as a set of control panels or devices that can help expand the use of your application. Because Motif runs in X, the capability to run multiple application windows at one time makes it possible to run modeless dialog boxes while continuing to work in the application window.

Dialog boxes can be designed in a variety of sizes and can be designed to any aspect ratio that will best convey the relevant functionality to the user. A good rule of thumb is to avoid making dialog boxes that are larger than their application windows. This could cause the user to be confused as to which window is the application and which window is the dialog box. Most users expect dialog boxes to be smaller than their

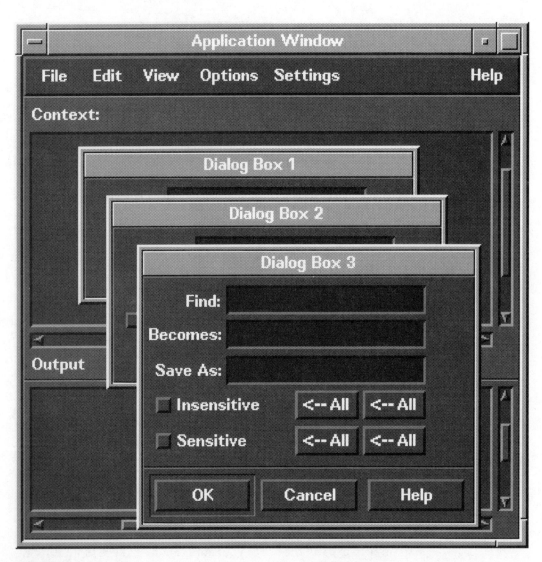

FIGURE 9–1 Each dialog box should be positioned to display itself at a stepped interval from the previous one.

application windows. Some early analysis as to which dialog boxes will be used together can help determine their visual layout. This will help to maximize the limited screen real estate whenever a combination of dialog boxes is displayed at the same time.

Dialog boxes can take many forms and use many layouts; however, almost all fall into one of four basic types. These types are characterized by the Pushbuttons that are in their respective confirmation rows: OK/Cancel, Apply/Undo/Close, OK, and Close. According to OSF compliance, all confirmation rows except for OK and Close incorporate Help as the last item situated at the right. Let's take a look at each type.

The OK/Cancel Dialog Box

The OK/Cancel dialog box is useful for confirming changes in settings; the changes can be evidenced after the user has confirmed the change by pressing the OK button. This type of confirmation allows the user to make changes to state settings or functions without getting into trouble if a wrong selection was made. Until the user selects the OK button, nothing will have changed. A user can force the dialog box to ignore any changes by pressing the Cancel button. The Cancel button should unpost the dialog box and not invoke any selected changes. This type of confirmation is useful for changes that are predictable. Usually, as these changes are invoked by pressing the OK button, the dialog box should automatically unpost itself and disappear. This change will be apparent at a later time.

An example of this type is the Session Startup dialog box in HP's VUE 2.0. This dialog box asks the user how to save the current session when shutting down the system. Three choices of how to save the current session are displayed for the user to select. One will always be selected as a result of the last time this dialog box was used. If a new selection was made, this change will not be evident until the next time the system is started. This is fine with the user because the three choices are predictable and can be evidenced when the system is started at a later time. Figure 9–2 shows the Session Startup dialog box that incorporates OK/Cancel.

The Apply/Close Dialog Box

The Apply/Close dialog box is slightly different. It is designed to apply changes immediately. The change is usually evident immediately somewhere on the screen. By invoking the Apply button, the user commits to

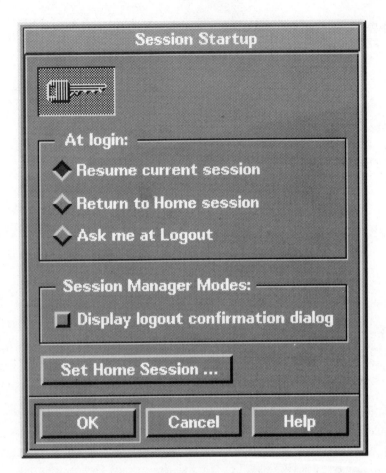

FIGURE 9–2 An example of an OK/Cancel dialog box.

any change in the dialog box. An Undo button should be incorporated with an Apply button whenever possible. If the change is not satisfactory, it can be reversed by pressing the Undo Pushbutton. If the user has a way to reverse the change by reselecting the previous choice, an Undo Pushbutton is not necessary. This will allow the user to reverse the last applied change. If an Undo Pushbutton is incorporated, it will undo the last selection or change invoked. This means that Undo could also undo an Undone invocation. This could be handy for quickly flipping back and forth between your selections. This dialog box is good for making changes in selections that are not as predictable as those for which the OK/Cancel dialog box is used. A selection made using the Apply Pushbutton should display the change immediately.

The Backdrop selector in HP's VUE 2.0 is an example of an Apply/Close dialog box. By using this dialog box, users can select a new backdrop pattern for the current workspace environment. They can scroll through the list to select a new pattern. The new selection is displayed in the view window in the dialog box. If the user decides to apply the displayed selection to the screen background, it is done by pressing the Apply default button. The background of the screen changes instantly to the new pattern. Because this dialog box is designed with a list selection window, the previous choice can be reapplied to the background if the user decides that the new pattern is not agreeable. Thus, an Undo button is not required. This type of dialog box should not unpost itself until the Close button is pressed. Figure 9–3 shows the Backdrop selection dialog box, which incorporates Apply/Close.

FIGURE 9–3 An example of an Apply/Close dialog box.

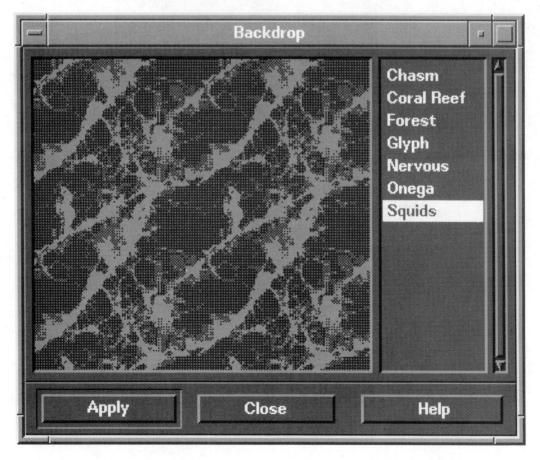

The OK Dialog Box

The OK dialog box should be used as a confirmation of a message or a warning. It is simply a reply to the system indicating that you have read and understood the message. Dialog boxes that display an OK confirmation should be modal, requiring the user to respond to them before resuming work with the system. This type of dialog box should be used to convey warnings or critical information that the user needs to know before continuing on. Figure 9–4 shows a warning dialog box incorporating only OK.

FIGURE 9–4 An example of an OK only dialog box.

The Close Dialog Box

The Close dialog box should be used when monitoring data. It can also be used as a display of captured images or as an advertisement for a product. When it is used as a display device, it is not critical for the system to know whether the user has read the display message. No state-setting selections or warnings or messages should be used with this type of dialog box. Users simply have to close the dialog box whether or not they have read it. When Close is pressed, the dialog box should unpost itself and disappear from the screen. Examples of uses for the Close dialog box could be Xload status windows or a clock function. Figure 9–5 shows a dialog box incorporating only Close.

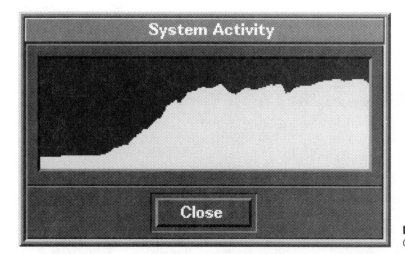

FIGURE 9–5 An example of a Close only dialog box.

Widget Layout in
Dialog Boxes

Dialog box widget layout spacing should be more generous than widget spacing in application windows. Because dialog boxes are usually smaller and temporary, they can warrant additional space between widgets in order to allow them not to appear too small. A good rule of thumb is to space widgets in dialog boxes twice as far apart as in application windows. Application windows usually require space efficiency in order to provide the user with the maximum work area possible, so their widgets are placed as close as possible to one another. Dialog boxes, on the other hand, are temporary and should not be designed like large windows fighting for space efficiency. They can have widgets spaced apart more generously. Figure 9–6 shows widget spacing in an application window compared with widget spacing in a dialog box.

Dialog boxes can have various visual characteristics. Dialog box designs should be a result of the functions that they are required to display. Figures B–4 and B–5 (color section) show a variety of dialog boxes that were designed for the Style Manager customization tool in HP's VUE 2.0.

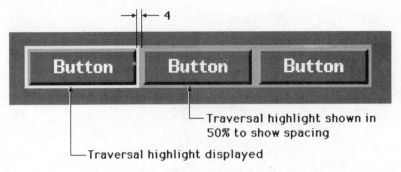

Application widget spacing

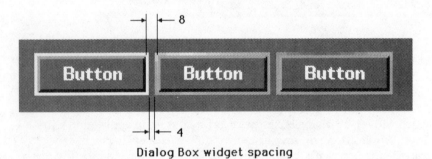

Dialog Box widget spacing

Traversal highlight thickness set to 2 pixels for this example.

FIGURE 9–6 Widget spacing in an application window should be closer and more space-efficient than widget spacing in a dialog box. Dialog boxes can afford to have widgets spaced farther apart from each other.

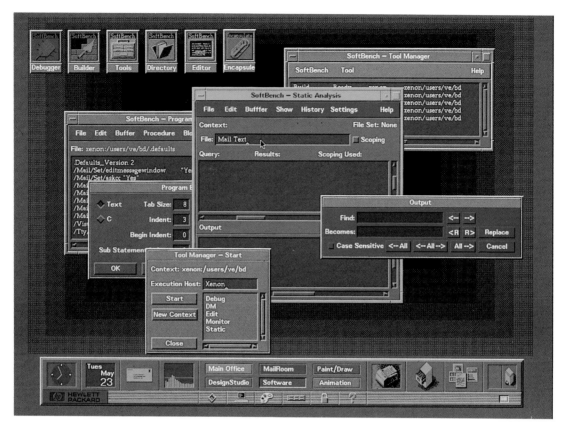

FIGURE C-1 The visual design of a multiwindowed environment should accommodate various applications. This example of HP SoftBench in HP VUE 2.0 shows that color harmony, as well as visual quality, should be consistent in order to create a unified appearance.

FIGURE C-2 In the File Manager in HP VUE 2.0, files, directories, and executables are visually represented by manipulable icons as described in chapter 6. A user can easily reorganize files and directories by direct manipulation.

FIGURE C–3 Personal customizing of each workspace is easily done in HP VUE 2.0. A variety of color schemes and background patterns can be chosen and applied to the screen environment. In this way, each workspace can have its own unique appearance and can help a user better remember each workspace's content by color and pattern association.

FIGURE C–4 New technologies for the workstation will require interface configurations that will facilitate user operation as well as product distinction. The ViewPhone shown here was taken from the HP video "1995." When designing this videophone, many design issues associated with the user's dialog and such a device were revealed.

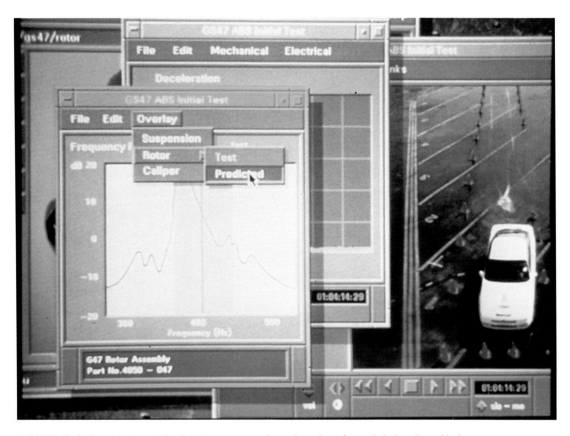

FIGURE C-5 Scenario-based visual design concepts show the value of a well-designed graphical user interface. Here is an example of conceptual video playback and measurement application windows working together to analyze a brake failure on a test car. This conceptual scenario from HP's video "1992" helped explore design issues surrounding simultaneous use of multiple applications.

FIGURE C–6 Multimedia is the current hot topic, which promises an integration of dissimilar technologies for the presentation of a common message. Technologies such as video, audio, animation, and real-time-shared working screens will require extensive analysis in order to design logical as well as appealing visual interfaces.

FIGURE C–7 The promise of the fully electronic office is almost here. The visual three-dimensional nature of Motif can be extended to represent other frequently used functions as familiar objects. This is one of Steve Anderson's many investigations into how an electronic office based on Motif could appear.

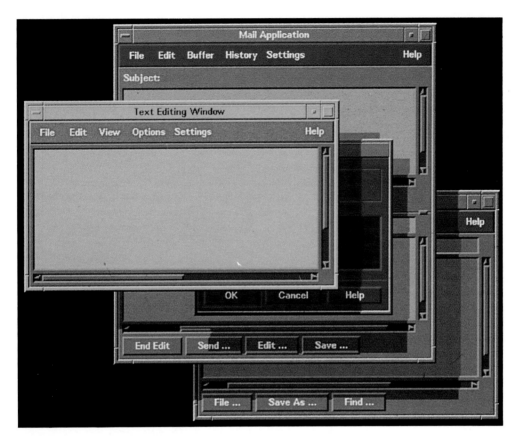

FIGURE C–8 The three-dimensional visual quality of Motif has taken us one step further toward a more realistic screen environment. Further enhancement of this three-dimensional quality can be obtained with the use of atmospheric perspective; this is when the application windows seem to recess into the background. The visual result is achieved when each subsequent window is slightly grayer than the one in front of it. Smart shadows can also be used to cast shadows of windows onto other windows. These shadows would convey the terrain of the three-dimensional widgets for each application.

Where Are We Headed?

Where are we headed with Motif as a graphical user interface? The future of Motif will be greatly influenced by the demands that users place on this GUI. Motif will have to continue to evolve its capabilities according to market demands. The future of Motif is being shaped and reshaped continuously as users' expectations change and develop. To be ready for the future and its demands, Motif's well-established foundation of behavior and aesthetic consistency will serve as a base from which future functionality will be designed. Consistency is very important, because users will rely on past experiences with other applications in order to try new applications. Based on this foundation, a variety of new innovative applications can be designed. The basic set of widgets outlined in this book will serve as the building blocks for ever more sophisticated applications. As users continue to become familiar with the Presentation Manager style of user interface behavior and Motif's three-dimensional appearance, they will be able to understand and use much more sophisticated application designs without the steep learning curve such programs would require today.

Present Applications

We have been involved with the visual design of new capabilities based on Motif. We at HP have somewhat extended the capabilities of Motif to its present limits with the HP Softbench CASE (Computer Aided Software Engineering) integration architecture as well as HP VUE 2.0 (Visual User Environment) direct manipulation environment. We have also developed file management capabilities as well as intuitive ways of customizing the screen environment based on Motif's GUI.

Softbench

Softbench is developed by HP's SESD (Software Engineering Systems Division: Chuck House, General Manager and Tom Christian, Lab Manager). HP's Softbench integrates a suite of software development tools that are most often needed for designing new applications or encapsulating existing ones. Its suite of tools has been designed based on Motif's three-dimensional interface model. Figure C–1 (color section) shows Softbench running in HP's VUE 2.0.

HP VUE 2.0

HP VUE (Visual User Environment) File Manager has been developed in concert with the Visual Design team at SESD, including Barry Mathis, Steve Anderson, and myself, in conjunction with the engineering team at ITO (Interface Technologies Operation: Chung Tung, General Manager; Ted Wilson, Lab Manager; and Bob Miller, Project Manager). The File Manager window allows direct manipulation of files represented in iconic form. Manipulation of the icons is based on an HP-developed drag-and-drop behavior. This allows for intuitive and direct manipulation of files. Figure C–2 (color section) shows the File Manager existing in HP's VUE 2.0

Ease of customization of the display screen has been a desire from the beginning with Motif. The Style Manager customization suite of applications has been developed by the Visual Design team of Barry Mathis, Steve Anderson, and myself with the engineering team at ITO (Chung Tung, General Manager; Ted Wilson, Lab Manager; and Ione Crandell, Project Manager). This suite of customization tools allows a user to change such things as colors, font sizes, and background patterns by direct manipulation of the controls displayed in each dialog box. There is no need to reenter the resource file just to change a background color. Everything is available to the user through direct manipulation. Figure C–3 (color section) shows the Style Manager in HP VUE 2.0.

Product Differentiation

As we continue to use Motif as the GUI in multiwindowed environments, there will be an ever-increasing number of applications fighting for your attention. The battle for your attention will not occur in your display but before you even buy your application. As in any pervasive technology, the desire for product differentiation and unique identity will increase. This unique identity provides a side benefit helping users identify the application that they are searching for on the computer screen.

As more powerful functionality become available, customer demand will increase for these technologies. As is expected, prices for these capabilities will undoubtedly be high at first. Customers who will be paying for these new capabilities in the future will demand a sense of satisfaction from their purchase. They will want their application to be the best and the most capable, and this should show in the application's visual design. Customers will become increasingly intolerant of applications with no thought put into their visual design. Visual design of applications not only will enhance their use but also will be used as a selling device for market appeal.

User-designed Applications

The future will empower the user with more capabilities than we have ever dreamed possible. Along with all this capability will come greater demands and expectations by the user. Users will expect total control and vast capabilities in their computing environment. The current set of widgets will become the equivalent of the screws, nuts, and bolts in today's mechanical world. The user will want to be more creative. The creativity that I am talking about here is not just the creative expression of a finished product, such as a document, drawing, or animation, but the creation of new powerful personal capabilities for the computer system. The user will demand capabilities that are not offered in applications and will want the capability to create these functions. The industrial revolution has spawned not just consumers (users) but inventors (developers) as well. There are more garage inventors today than ever in human history. This is simply a result of evolution and the gradual understanding by more and more people of everyday mechanical devices. The same evolution will continue to occur in the information revolution as more people become exposed to the capabilities and shortcomings of computers.

People will want to invent new functionalities, not only for profit or fame but from a desire to take creative control of a new technology. From this will come an increasing number of user-designed applications.

Some may be individual concoctions with limited appeal, and others will have mass appeal and could benefit the existing GUI offering. Builder applications that are easy to use and understand will play a crucial role in the development of user-designed applications by everyday people. Builders are applications that allow people with minimal programming knowledge to develop an application with standard widgets.

Interaction with New Technologies

Whenever new technologies enter our lives, we as a society must deal with them in the best way possible without succumbing to fear, intimidation, or embarrassment. We often rely on past experiences to figure out the best way to accept any new technology in our lives. Reliance on socially accepted customs and etiquette for dealing with the use of new devices has been the norm with most people. There will always be some trepidation when people are trying a new technology for the first time. While Motif and other GUIs attempt to break down these barriers, there will continue to be progress for new capabilities. The question of how to interact with these new technologies has a great effect on us personally. These social perceptions with new technology become design interaction problems for the application developer to solve when designing an application. The use of an interactive whiteboard, for instance, will reveal not only the technological questions but just as importantly its interaction questions. The latter is just as important as the former and will be the key to whether this new technology will be accepted by users.

New social behaviors and etiquettes will be defined with any new technology. For instance, a shared whiteboard will require users at either end of the conversation to find a way to communicate in such a way that they are not writing or drawing over each other's ideas at the same time. There might be time delays, and patience must be exercised to have a productive meeting.

For instance, since the telephone was invented, a whole set of social behaviors just for talking on the telephone has evolved. Over the years people have accepted the fact that it is okay to talk into this device called a telephone; however, take away the handset and all of a sudden it would be just as awkward to talk with nothing in your hand as it used to be to talk into the handset. Society, over time, develops its own acceptable and unacceptable standards of behavior. New technologies using the computer will again challenge these perceptions.

Specialized Domain-specific Widgets

As more and more people rely on the computer for their daily professional tasks, domain-specific functionality will increase. The uses for the computer are almost limitless, and domain-specific applications will be in high demand in the future. People will grow increasingly less tolerant of using generic applications for their specific tasks. Today spreadsheet applications are used for more diverse functions than even the application writer probably imagined. Similarly, many paint programs are used for designing as well as painting, word processing programs are used for typesetting as much as for writing letters. People seek out specialized functionality, and when there is no specifically designed application available, they will make do with whatever is out there, only to long for the perfect set of functions one day.

Future Concepts Based on Motif's Three-Dimensional Visual Design

ViewPhone
Communication

There will come a time when cooperative computing will be as normal a mode of communication as the telephone is today. Visual communications via the computer screen will open up a world of communications capabilities that were never available before. As tasks increasingly must be tended to while communicating, there will be an increasing need to be able to quickly identify and operate functions while communicating on a ViewPhone. The quality of the visual design of these applications' user interfaces will be crucial to the ease of use of a device as complex and as dynamic as live video communication.

Visual design details such as screen size, control size, and ease of identification can be either convenient or annoying to the user. The user must have immediate access to numerous functions, such as volume and brightness controls. These types of controls must be designed to be recognized quickly and easily manipulable.

The image in figure C–4 (color section) shows a clip from Hewlett Packard's future vision video entitled "1995." We've designed a conceptual video telephone for the workstation screen environment. The design called for quick visual identification of the Viewphone application as well as a vanity window below in which users can see themselves while interacting via video means. Controls such as brightness, volume, and transporter access were identified as being important for quick and easy access while conversing.

The ViewPhone warranted some visual product differentiation, because it is a unique application that will be pervasive throughout your environment. The rounding off of the view window, as well as the design of a smaller subwindow underneath was an experiment to see if the functions in a unique window will still be recognizable.

The use of the Viewphone revealed some interesting social problems. One was that of transmitting a document to the people to whom users were talking. The other was the users' need to know if they are in focus and look presentable. When we designed the Viewphone, the script called for a document to be sent from one caller to the other during the conversation. At that time, the popular convention was to place the document on the Viewphone screen, at which point the document will somehow mysteriously transmit itself to the person on the other end. We felt this to be rude to the other person. It felt as though we were shoving the document in the other person's face. Instead, we came up with the idea of the transporter. The transporter is a dedicated part of the interface through which documents can be sent and retrieved. It provides the user a discreet method of real-time transmission of files.

The Viewphone will also change our communication habits. Our need to know if we are presentable is a very real problem that must be dealt with when designing a tool like this. The Vanity window was an idea that allowed the user to see if he/she was visually presentable, with quick access to zooming controls as well as an instant means of turning off the transmission of your image or simply closing the vanity window altogether.

These social interaction problems become design problems and must be taken into account when designing a visual interface. These examples were designed as a result of this complex nature of real time interaction with a live person at the other end.

Video Playback Windows

When video playback and authoring become pervasive in the computing environment, Motif's three-dimensional interface can provide a clear visual differentiation between the video image and its playback mechanisms. In a multiwindowed environment, a videotape can be viewed while measurements are taken on a chart that describes the subject matter being played in the video. The conceptual video window shown in figure C–5 (color section) was designed to follow proper Motif design guidelines with its Menubar at the top. Its Video display window is in the center of the window displaying the video, and its controls were placed at the bottom so that the operation of the video window wouldn't obstruct the viewing window.

Controls for this window were designed to be displayed in the open at the bottom of the window so that users can have quick access to the controls without needing to pull down a Menupane for each function. Pull-down Menus for functions during the viewing of a video will obstruct the video image. Other controls, such as brightness and volume, were placed up front as well, because these controls often must be adjusted during playback of a video.

Multimedia and Cooperative Shared Whiteboard

There has been much talk of multimedia and how it is going to change and enhance our use of computers. Multimedia promises to bring new capabilities as well as to enhance our working experience with computers. This is all very exciting. The challenge in multimedia will be from the application developer's perspective. The visual interaction alone contains enough questions to keep you busy for a long time. Questions related to authoring tools, libraries of images, sound, animation, etc. will keep the patent and trademark lawyers busy for decades. Even if the technology were here today, there would be a lot of time spent on the How questions. How will the user use this? Figure C–6 (color section) shows a concept of a multimedia environment that uses a sound annotated document, a video playback window, a ViewPhone, and a shared whiteboard to tackle a task.

The Office

Much of the talk about using Graphical User Interfaces centers around the capability to design and use a virtual office, complete with all the symbols and amenities of an office. The Motif visual design model allows us to explore what the computer office of the future might be like. Perhaps our computer office will incorporate familiar storage devices such as file cabinets, shelves, and drawers. In the physical world, we are constantly keeping track of hundreds of items without much effort. We tend to know by size, shape, color, and placement where most of our personal artifacts are located in our offices as well as in our homes. The computer screen can be designed to emulate this situation using Motif's GUI. This could provide an intuitive screen environment for most users who are much more comfortable manipulating images of familiar devices than trying to associate an abstraction with a function. Figure C–7 (color section) shows a concept by user interface designer Steve Anderson of what a future virtual office may look like.

Atmospheric Perspective and Smart Shadows

The notion of atmospheric perspective has intrigued us for quite some time now. Atmospheric perspective is a natural phenomenon in our world — the atmosphere of our planet makes distant objects look faded and less detailed, whereas objects that are closer appear saturated and highly detailed. This natural phenomenon allows us to judge distance and realize which objects are in front of others. The notion of smart shadows also adds to this realism. The smart shadow is an idea that we have come up with to help us judge distance. As in the real world, shadows are cast by objects onto other objects by the light source, whether it is the sun or an artificial light. Shadows help us determine the time of day as well as the angle of an object relative to the light source. Shadows also help us determine whether one object is in front of another. *Smart Shadows* is a term we coined for transparent shadows that are cast by one window over another and that would understand the terrain of the three-dimensional components of the window underneath. The shadow would appear to display itself accurately by displaying the peaks and valleys of the interface as well as by revealing its height above another window by the size of the shadow cast onto the lower window. These concepts, based on Motif's visual principles, would serve as visual cues to make the three-dimensional screen environment look as realistic as possible. Figure C–8 (color section) shows an example of HP's patented Smart Shadows.

Glossary

6-bit display card: A computer monitor display circuit card that enables the computer to display 64 colors at a time on the screen.

8-bit display card: A computer monitor display circuit card that enables the computer to display 256 colors at a time on the screen.

64 colors: The number of colors that can be displayed at once on a computer screen whose system uses a 6-bit display card.

256 colors: The number of colors that can be displayed at once on a computer screen whose system uses an 8-bit display card.

active input focus: A window state indicating that this window has the keyboard input focus to the exclusion of the other windows. Its window frame will highlight with a bright color to indicate this state.

API: Application Program Interface.

application window: The window in which an application resides with its complete user interface.

armed: The state of a widget just before being invoked. See also *selected.*

ascent: The height of the character of the font above the font's baseline.

atmospheric perspective: The effect of distance created by using paler and less intense color for faraway elements, representing them as they appear in nature owing to conditions of distance, air, and light.

background: The flat area on which a widget resides. Also the flat area of the widget that is colored with the dominant color of the widget.

background color: The color from which all widgets create their top and bottom shadows and their select color, and against which labels and bitmaps are created with the foreground color.

baseline: A reference line placed in a font that divides the font character into its ascent and descent areas.

bit: The smallest unit of information, which maps either the background or the foreground color to a single pixel.

bitmap: An image created by using only two colors of the screen.

bloom: A human visual effect, in which light colors on the screen tend to expand into the surrounding darker colors. For example, a white-on-black letter will look thicker than a black-on-white letter. This natural effect is a result of the eye averaging a pattern of contrasting values.

bottom shadow: The darkest color of a widget, calculated from the background color.

card: Refers to a display circuit board in a computer.

chamfer: The frame surrounding most widgets that gives them their three-dimensional appearance. Also referred to as *top and bottom shadows.*

character cell: The area surrounding the font glyphs which the widgets recognize. All widget resource dimensions start from the outside edges of the character cell.

child: A hierarchical reference to widgets. A child widget can be either a primitive or a manager widget. The term implies that the child widget requires a parent widget to control it.

client: Any widget or a set of widgets that is configured to be displayed in a window.

client manager: The functional area in a window that contains and has responsibility for all of the window's widgets.

code: The set of programmatic commands that translate the widget callbacks into understandable computer functions.

color cell: The individual place holder for each color displayed on the screen.

color-code: A coding mechanism that is created by using various colors for individual functional areas.

color map: A reference of the entire set of colors that can be displayed at one time by the computer.

color server: The computer servicing the color requests of each running and displayed application.

color values: The Red, Green, and Blue (RGB) numbers that define an exact color to the computer: three numbers, one each for Red, Green, and Blue, from 0 to 63 for 6-bit display cards and from 0 to 255 for 8-bit display cards.

command: A string that acts as a function.

confirmation row: The row of buttons at the bottom of a dialog box. For example: OK, Cancel, Help.

contrast: The amount of visual distinction between color values; the greater the contrast, the clearer the image.

CRT: Cathode ray tube. Otherwise known as a *display screen.*

CUA: Common User Access. IBM's prescribed graphical user interface behavior guidelines for computer systems.

CXI: Common X Interface. The original name of the three-dimensional widgets before they were adopted as OSF's Motif.

descent: The distance the font character glyph extends below the font's baseline.

diacritical mark: A modifying mark near or through a character or a combination of characters showing phonetic values different from those given to unmarked characters.

dialog box: A subwindow that is spawned by the application when detailed or overly abundant information needs to be displayed or acquired.

direct manipulation: The capability to grab and move objects or invoke functions on the screen by interacting with the objects themselves as opposed to using commands.

display: The manifestation of application information on the screen. In other words, the appearance of the application on the screen. Also, in hardware terms, display is the physical computer monitor.

dithered: Various patterns created by using two or more colors to achieve a new color effect in the viewer's eyes.

domain: A specific profession or area of interest.

ergonomics: The physical and psychological relationship between the workstation or its interface and a human.

executable: A file in computer readable code; a program.

explicit: A mode in which the mouse must be pressed in an application window in order for the window to recognize that it has the keyboard input focus to the exclusion of other windows. As a result, the application will have the active input focus. See also *implicit*.

file: A document that has been created and stored in memory or on a disk.

file manager: An application that contains, organizes, and opens and closes files.

file window: The viewable window of the file manager.

fixed pitch font: A font in which all character cells occupy identical widths as measured in pixels.

font: A complete assembly of all of the characters of one size of one typeface, including capitals, lowercase characters, figures, punctuation marks, and reference marks.

foreground: The name given to the color of the components, such as labels and pixmaps, that are usually placed against the background color.

form: The shape of an object, whether in physical space or on a computer's screen.

gadgets: Higher performing versions of widgets designed without the overhead involved in having each widget have its own window. Visually identical to widgets.

glyphs: The pixel patterns that make up the visual characters of a font.

gray scale: A set of neutral gray tones ranging from light to dark without any apparent color hues attached to them.

GUI: Graphical user interface: A visual representation of a computer's functions that are manipulable by nonprogrammatic means.

hardware: The physical parts of a computer workstation.

hue: The various colors of the spectrum visible to the human eye, such as red, yellow, green, blue, etc.

icon: A graphic image that represents either an application that has been miniaturized and is running or a file that is closed and not running in a file manager window. Pictograms that serve as symbols in lieu of a Label are also referred to as Icons.

Icon Box: An application that will store and visually organize the icons of applications that are minimized and running.

implicit: A mode in which a window recognizes that it has the keyboard input focus to the exclusion of other windows as soon as the mouse is moved into the window; the mouse button does not have to be pressed. See also *explicit*.

inactive input focus: The state of a displayed window that does not have the keyboard input focus to the exclusion of other windows.

insensitive: A state that a widget can be in when it does not have any useful function in a given functional scenario. An insensitive widget's Label will be filled with a dithered pattern and will appear grayed out.

interface: The layer of graphically displayed information between the user and the computer.

invert: To reciprocate two colors, usually the foreground and background, in order to highlight a selected widget.

invoke: To implement a function in an application or a dialog box.

Label: The text or pixmap placed in a widget that describes the widget's function. The term *Label* is also used for the words used to describe an area or function.

launching: The action by the computer that brings up a file with its associated application.

lighting model: An established set of artistic rules that prescribes where the simulated light is shining from. This ensures consistent top and bottom shadows for each widget.

luminosity: The amount of lightness or darkness associated with a color or hue. Also referred to as *value* or *brightness.*

manager: A hierarchical term used to describe widgets that can contain and have responsibility for other primitive and manager widgets.

Matte: A three-dimensional visual border surrounding a bitmapped image or a view of a document inside of a window frame.

maximize: The action that allows a window to expand and fill the entire screen.

minimize: The action that allows a window to miniaturize into an icon while continuing to run.

mode: A functional state determined by a set of changes made to a particular widget.

monitor: The computer device that houses the display screen.

monochrome: A video terminal capable of showing images in only one hue and its derivative values. Usually black and white.

MS-DOS: Microsoft's Disk Operating System. An operating system that is different from UNIX.

muted: A term used to describe soft desaturated colors that result in a sort of grayish tone.

n **of many:** A state to which a toggle can be set in which more than one of a set of choices can be selected at any time.

neutral: A visual characteristic of colors that can be matched with a variety of other colors.

one-of-many: A state to which a toggle can be set in which only one of a set of choices can be selected at any time.

outline: A description of character glyphs using enveloping control points. This technology is used to resize fonts into an infinite variety of sizes that still appear visually pleasing.

palette: A set of visually compatible colors.

parent: A hierarchical term used for widgets that can contain and have responsibility for other primitive or manager widgets.

pixel values: A measurement in screen pixels used to determine sizes of widget elements.

platform: An association of hardware, operating system, peripheral, and library software that defines a distinct computing environment.

pointer: An alternate term used to describe a mouse cursor.

polychromatic: Used to describe a color whose characteristics are a result of a combination of different colors mixed together. Often described as grayish blue or pinkish green.

ppi: Refers to the screen's visual density in pixels per inch. Also known as *dpi* (dots per inch).

> *72 ppi:* The number of pixels in an inch on the screen. 72 ppi means that there are 72 pixels in a linear inch on the computer screen.

> *120 ppi:* The number of pixels in an inch on the screen. 120 ppi means that there are 120 pixels in a linear inch on the computer screen.

Presentation Manager: A graphical user interface toolkit based on IBM's CUA (Common User Access) behavioral standards.

primitive: A hierarchical term used to describe widgets that cannot contain and have responsibility for other primitive or manager widgets.

quad: A set of four related colors that make up a widget's colors. These are usually background, top shadow, bottom shadow, and select colors.

redraw: The action of a computer when it recreates an image on the screen.

requests: Commands that are sent from an application to the server asking for a specific function or attribute.

resource: An attribute or a property of a widget that must be assigned a value or a specification.

RGB: Red, Green, and Blue. The Red, Green, and Blue picture guns in each of a computer's monitor pixels. The varying intensity of each gun's emission onto the screen provides the wide variety of displayed color.

sans serif fonts: The typeface category that includes fonts that do not feature any serifs. See also *serif fonts.*

saturated: Very strong intensity in color without any visual hint of dilution.

scroll: The action of moving through a document line by line or by other increments. This term is taken from the metaphor of a continuous scroll that is to be read through a viewing window.

select color: The slightly darker color variation based on the background color of a widget. This is not as dark as the bottom shadow color.

selected state: The momentary or permanent state of a widget resulting from the action of pressing on a widget in order to invoke a function or to change a setting.

serif fonts: Fonts that include serifs, the finishing strokes at the ends of letters that contribute to the recognizability of individual characters. Serifs are believed to increase readability; such fonts are best suited for extended reading.

server: A computer servicing requests for information processing or information display.

shadows: The light and dark chamfers surrounding most widgets to provide a three-dimensional appearance. Shadows are referred to in this book as *top and bottom shadows.*

slab: A visual result of chamfering the edges of a colored area with top and bottom shadows. The result is a visual thickness of the background of the interface.

sprite: An alternate term used for the mouse cursor.

state: A condition or a mode of a widget or icon

when selected or invoked.

string: Text or a line of text that is used for labeling a widget.

system area: Any area in an application window or a dialog box or other parts of a GUI in which the user cannot manipulate or edit data. See also *user area.*

system font: The style of font recommended for use in all system areas. See also *user font.*

three-dimensional: Refers to the appearance of an image that appears to have real physical form and mass.

tint: An alternate term used to describe a color's hue. To change a tint of a color is to alter its actual color.

top shadow: The lightest color of a widget, derived from the background color.

traversal highlight: A visual highlight that appears on or around most widgets to indicate that this widget has the mouse or keyboard focus to the exclusion of other widgets in the window.

traverse: The action of moving from widget to widget via the keyboard or with the mouse. Also see *keyboard traversal.*

trough: The depressed channel in a Scale or Scrollbar widget.

tweak: A term used to express the process of making very minute adjustments.

two-dimensional: Refers to a flat appearance of an image—the visual effect does not attempt to hint at the object's real physical form.

UIL: User Interface Language. Digital Equipment Corporation's language for textually describing widget layout and behavior.

unarmed: The visual state of a widget that is unselected.

UNIX: An operating system licensed by AT&T.

user area: Any area in an application window or a dialog box in which the user can manipulate or edit data.

user font: The style of font recommended for user areas in which the user is able to enter, manipulate, or edit data, or to select data that has been edited in the past.

valuator: The dynamically changing bar that resides within a Scrollbar. The valuator indicates the amount of data currently in view relative to the entire amount of data. It is also used as a handle to scroll through the data.

value: A numerical or text specification assigned to widget resources. In reference to color, value also means the amount of lightness or darkness of a particular color.

variable pitch font: A variable spacing method used for allocating widths to font glyphs in proportion to the ideal width of characters. Also known as proportional spacing.

widget: An industry standard term used as a generic name for graphical user interface components.

Window Manager: The underlying application that enables windows to be displayed and directly manipulated on the screen.

workstation: A multitasking personal computer system.

WYSIWYG: "What You See Is What You Get." A term used in the desktop publishing industry for trying to match the appearance of the information on the display with the appearance of the printed output.

X: A portable, networked transparent window system.

Xm: The prefix Xm is placed before any value that is specified as a widget resource. A convention that identifies the X window system and Motif values as different from other values found in source code.

XmN: The prefix XmN is placed before any resource classification that requires a specified value.

Bibliography

Molenkamp, Jan and Center, Stu, *Type Terms*. Hewlett Packard, 1989.

Open Software Foundation. *Application Environment Specification, User Environment Volume*. Prentice Hall, 1990.

Open Software Foundation. *OSF/Motif User's Guide*. Prentice Hall, 1990.

Schneiderman, Ben. *Designing the User Interface*. Addison-Wesley, 1987.

Smith, Wanda. *Using Computer Color Effectively*. Prentice Hall, 1989.

Young, Douglas. *The X Window System Programming and Applications with Xt OSF/MOTIF Edition*. Prentice Hall, 1990.

Index

2-bit display card, 20
6-bit display card
  color map for, 11–12, *13*
  colors/gray shades available with, 20
8-bit display card, 20
64 colors, 11–12, *13*
256 colors, 19

Active input focus, 168–169, A-8
Alignment
  in option menus, 116, *117*
  of pushbuttons, 59, *61*
  of text, in labels, *50*, 51, *52*, 53, *54*, *55*
API (Application Program Interface), 1
Application(s)
  development of future, based on three-dimensionality, 233–236

differentiation of, in the future, 231
manipulating on-screen (*see* Window Manager)
with paned windows, 90, *93*
representation of, as icon, 182–183
specialized domain-specific, in the future, 233
user-designed, in the future, 231–232
Application design. *See also* Design principles; Layout principles
Application Program Interface (API), 1
Apply/Close dialog box, 223–225, *226*
Arrows, 73–74
  four alternate directions for, 73, *74*
  as gadget, 46
  pixmap, in pulldown menus, 109, 110, *111*
  as primitive widget, 44

Trademarks

Hewlett Packard and HP are trademarks of Hewlett Packard Company.

IBM is a trademark of International Business Machines Corporation.

Macintosh is a registered trademark of Apple Computer, Inc.

Microsoft and MS-DOS are registered trademarks of Microsoft Corporation.

Motif and OSF/Motif are trademarks of Open Software Foundation Inc.

NeWS is a registered trademark of Sun Microsystems.

Open Look is a registerted trademark of AT&T.

Presentation Manager is a trademark of International Business Machines Corporation.

Star and Viewpoint are trademarks of Xerox Corporation.

Windows is a trademark of Microsoft Corporation.

X Window System is a trademark of the Massachusetts Institute of Technology.

XUI is a trademark of Digital Equipment Corporation.

Unix is a registered trademark of AT&T Bell Laboratories.

About the Author

Shiz Kobara is a senior user interface designer in the Software Engineering Systems Division, managed by Chuck House, at Hewlett Packard Company in Sunnyvale, California. Shiz has 10 years of experience as an industrial designer involved with corporate wide industrial design coordination, engineering best practices, and product design and market analysis. During the past three years, Shiz has focused on the design of graphical user interfaces (GUIs) for Hewlett Packard's workstations.

Working with the engineering team at the Interface Technologies Operation (ITO) of Hewlett Packard, managed by Chung Tung, Shiz was responsible for conceptualizing and was instrumental in implementing the visual interface design for HP's CXI three-dimensional widgets. He was also involved in the adoption of this visual design as Open Software Foundation's Motif standard graphical user interface, and the visual design of HP's SoftBench Computer Aided Software Engineering (CASE) suite of tools. Together with Steve Anderson, under the design management of Barry Mathis, Shiz was responsible for the visual and behavioral design of Hewlett Packard's extension of the Motif GUI into HP VUE 2.0 (Visual User Environment) and the conceptual interface designs for HP's vision of the future entitled "1995." Shiz is actively involved on a continuing basis with ITO in designing the further visual and behavioral evolution of the Motif GUI for the Open Software Foundation.

Shiz is a native of California and grew up in San Francisco. He graduated from San Jose State University in 1981, earning a Bachelor of Science degree in industrial design. He joined Hewlett Packard in 1981 as an industrial designer and since 1987 has gone on to design graphical user interfaces.